SPEAKING OUR TRUTH

A Journey of Reconciliation

MONIQUE GRAY SMITH

ORCA BOOK PUBLISHERS

Cataloguing in Publication information available from Library and Archives Canada

ISBN 978-1-4598-1583-4 (hardcover).—ISBN 978-1-4598-1584-1 (PDF).—
ISBN 978-1-4598-1585-8 (EPUB)

First published in the United States, 2017
Library of Congress Control Number: 2017933028

Summary: This nonfiction book examines how we can foster reconciliation with
Indigenous people at individual, family, community and national levels.
For a teacher guide and other resources, go to speakingourtruth.ca.

*Orca Book Publishers is dedicated to preserving the environment and has
printed this book on Forest Stewardship Council ® certified paper.*

Orca Book Publishers gratefully acknowledges the support for its publishing programs
provided by the following agencies: the Government of Canada, the Canada Council for the Arts
and the Province of British Columbia through the BC Arts Council and the Book Publishing Tax Credit.

Edited by Sarah N. Harvey
Consulting Editor: Greg Younging
Design by Gerilee McBride

Front cover photo: iStock.com. Front inset photos, top to bottom: Three boys at Pelican Residential School near Sioux
Lookout, ON. (OA c330 13-0-0-162) St. Michael's Residential School entrance, with two students on the driveway,
Alert Bay, BC is shown in 1970. (LAC 3378417) In March, 2013 a group of Cree youth walked 1600 kilometers to bring
attention to aboriginal issues on Parliament Hill in Ottawa, ON. (Shutterstock.com) Cree drummer Theland Kicknosway
(Fred Catroll) Jingle dancers take part in a Pow Wow in Kahnawake, QC, 2016. (Shutterstock.com)
Back cover photo: Dancers participate in annual Squamish Nation Pow Wow
on July 10, 2010 in West Vancouver, BC (iStock.com)

Author photo: Centric Photography

ORCA BOOK PUBLISHERS
orcabook.com

Printed and bound in Canada.

22 21 20 19 • 8 7 6 5

For my mom, Shirley Smith, whose strength
and resilience are truly remarkable.

CONTENTS

‣1‣
WELCOME TO THE JOURNEY

{ **"Throughout this book there are beautiful teachings I have received on my journey. They come from my relatives, Elders, Residential School Survivors and the many other people who have shared their ideas and wisdom."**
Monique Gray Smith }

Everyone loves going on vacation, right? I know I do. Visiting family, camping, seeing new places, playing in the waves on a tropical beach…all of it can be fun!

So how is taking a journey different from going on a vacation? Well, for one thing, a journey doesn't always require a plane, a train, a bus or even a car. It does require an open mind and a kind heart, because when we go on a journey we are often attempting to understand something in a deeper way. A journey can include learning more about a country, a time period or a different culture, and it always includes learning about ourselves. Journeys usually change us. Sometimes the change may

◀ Photo: Shari Nakagawa

"Reconciliation begins with you."

Chief Dr. Robert Joseph, Gwawaenuk First Nation

reconciliation—the restoration and healing of a relationship. In Canada, this refers to the process taken on by the Truth and Reconciliation Commission to revitalize the relationship between the citizens of Canada (Indigenous and non-Indigenous), as well as the Nation-to-Nation relationships with the Government of Canada.

be so small that we hardly notice it, while at other times it dramatically shifts our thinking, our behaviour and how we look at our world.

In this book, we are embarking on a journey of **reconciliation**. This isn't a read-and-do-nothing kind of book. It is an active exploration of Canada's collective history, our present and our future. It's about how we grow as individuals, families, communities and as a country. For some of you, this may be a time of significant change in your understanding of Canada's history. It might be the first time you've thought about what reconciliation means and, more specifically, what it means to *you* and what your role in it is. Simply reading this book is an act of reconciliation. So, good on you! Some of you may have started the journey well before picking this book up. I welcome you all to the journey. In my Nihiyaw (Cree) language, we say *tawâw*, which loosely means "there's always room." For you, for me, for your friends, your family, your community. There's always room.

A family camps on their way to the Red Deer Industrial Institute. UCCA 93.049P/861N

WHY DO WE NEED THIS JOURNEY?

So...*why* do we need to go on a journey of reconciliation?

In order to answer this question, we must first understand what we are reconciling.

Until the last few years, most Canadians knew very little about Residential Schools. Young people like you were not taught about them in school, and in many cases neither were your parents or grandparents. Some people had never even heard about them. But for over 150 years, **Indigenous** children were taken from their homes and placed in Residential Schools.

You might wonder how this could happen in our country. Well, a lot of it had to do with **systemic racism**. Laws and government policies were passed that allowed **Indian agents** (who worked for what was then called the Department of Indian Affairs) and the RCMP to take children as young as five years old away from everyone they loved and everything that was familiar and important to them. They were taken from their families, homes and communities and away from their land, culture and language. If parents or families attempted to stop this, they could be arrested, and the children were still taken.

Indigenous—the term that is most commonly being used now to describe First Peoples, Métis and Inuit.

systemic racism—when systems (like schools or the justice system) are supported and maintained by policies, practices and procedures that result in some people receiving better or worse treatment than others because of their race.

Indian agent—the representative of the Department of Indian Affairs (now known as Indigenous and Northern Affairs Canada). Indian agents were in charge of many aspects of affairs in their area or on the reserve(s) they were assigned to. The powers of the Indian agent were significant and influenced the lives of First Nations people in their area.

The Red Deer Industrial Institute outside Red Deer, AB, was established in 1893.
UCCA 93.049P/839

For these children, the initial trauma of being away from family and loved ones was intensified by:

▸ Being separated from siblings and cousins or prevented from talking to siblings or cousins of a different gender.

▸ Being hungry. Children and staff received different meals. The children's food was not nourishing, and at times it was rotten and full of maggots.

▸ Being abused. Physical, verbal, emotional, sexual and spiritual abuse was commonplace in the schools.

▸ Being forbidden to speak their own language or practise their own spirituality.

Having their hair, which they often wore in long braids, cut—buzz cuts for the boys, and short bobs for the girls. (It is important to understand that in many Indigenous Nations, hair has significant meaning. The cutting of it often means there has been a death in the family. To children, most of whom did not speak English and did not understand why their hair was being cut, this experience was often traumatic.)

Being forced to wear different clothes. Often the new clothes were ill-fitting and not suited for the climate in which the school was located.

Discipline was not only abusive, but also communicated a message to the children that they were *less than*.

All of this caused the significant loss of traditional languages in families and communities. It also fostered **internalized racism**, which led to a lack of pride and honour in being an Indigenous person.

Because of the courage of Survivors—former students—and their families, we have begun to understand what happened at those schools and the ripple effect of those experiences, which is still being felt in families, communities and our country.

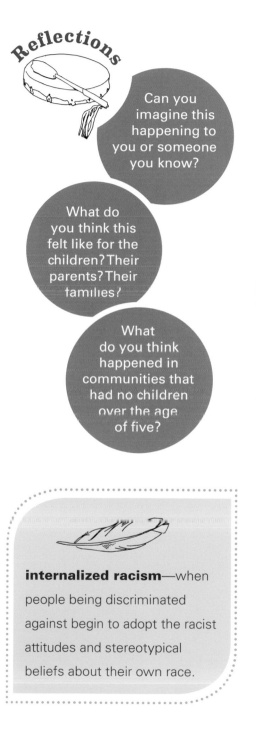

Reflections

Can you imagine this happening to you or someone you know?

What do you think this felt like for the children? Their parents? Their families?

What do you think happened in communities that had no children over the age of five?

internalized racism—when people being discriminated against begin to adopt the racist attitudes and stereotypical beliefs about their own race.

Let's start with some basic questions to help you reflect on your own knowledge and beliefs.

Do you know any Indigenous people?

Are you an Indigenous person? Is someone in your family Indigenous?

Whose territory is your school on?

Whose territory is your house on?

What do you know about the history of the territory where you live?

What do you know about the Indigenous people whose territory you live on?

Canada's relationship with Indigenous people has suffered as a result of Residential Schools as well as other legislative decisions that I will share with you in the next chapter of this book. Healing and repairing this relationship requires education, awareness, empathy and an increased understanding of the Residential School legacy.

It is time for the journey and the climbing to begin.

PREPARING FOR THE JOURNEY

What to Pack

For most trips you would pack a suitcase or back-pack with clothes, deodorant and a toothbrush. You *do* pack your toothbrush, don't you?

Because this journey is different, I'm asking you to pack simple things:

a willingness to listen to and have meaningful conversations with others

curiosity

openness

an ability to reflect on difficult things

What to Leave Behind

How often have you gone on a trip and only used half of what you packed? I do it all the time! There are certain things I encourage you to *unpack* before you head out on this journey. These aren't things like your toothbrush, extra shirts or extra shoes. They are thoughts, attitudes and maybe even beliefs, such as:

▸ I've heard all this before

▸ Reconciliation doesn't involve me, my friends or my family

▸ History isn't important

▸ I, as one person, can't make a difference

As a key part of your journey, you will find questions that encourage you to reflect on what you have learned. You'll read stories from young people, from Elders, from Residential School Survivors and their families, and from Canadians who love our country and are active in reconciliation. They have come together to share their perspectives, what they've learned about Residential Schools, what it means to be an **ally**, what reconciliation means to them and what they hope for Canada and all of its citizens.

> "As Commissioners we have described for you the mountain. We have shown you the path to the top. We call upon you to do the climbing."
> **Justice Murray Sinclair,**
> Chair, Truth and Reconciliation Commission of Canada

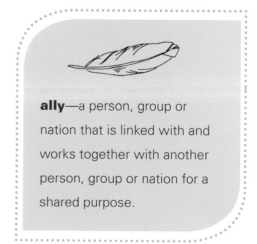

ally—a person, group or nation that is linked with and works together with another person, group or nation for a shared purpose.

Throughout history, different terms have been used to describe the first peoples of this land we now call Canada—*Indian, Native, First Nation, Aboriginal, Indigenous*. I tried to use the terms that were the norm at specific times. When talking about the late 1800s and early 1900s, for example, I use *Indian*. For the late 1980s I use *Aboriginal*, and in the context of the present day, I use *Indigenous*.

There are a number of interviews or portions of interviews woven throughout the book. Out of respect for the interviewees and their unique way of sharing, the interviews have not been edited.

Monique's Journey

It wouldn't be fair of me to ask you to go on a journey that I am not willing to go on myself. So I'm going to share with you a bit of what my journey has been like as I wrote this book.

When I was asked to write a book for young people about reconciliation, my first response was *no*. And not just a no, but *NO*! I was sitting at the kitchen table, working on my laptop, when the email arrived. I guess my head was moving back and forth, and I was saying, "No, no, no!" My partner asked me what I was saying no to so emphatically. I told her, but she couldn't understand why I wasn't jumping at the opportunity.

I have been sharing Canadian history from an Indigenous perspective since the year 2000, and I

Monique at age ten.

have always worked to foster relationships between Indigenous and non-Indigenous people. I watched the work of the Truth and Reconciliation Commission with keen interest. I guess you can say I'm a student of reconciliation. Maybe you can see why my partner was confused. But inside my head, yelling at me through a loudspeaker, was the voice of doubt. *Why me? Who am I to write this book?*

You see, part of my inner turmoil was because my own ancestry is both **colonizer** and **colonized**. So what does that mean? It means I am of both Indigenous and non-Indigenous ancestry. It means I have family who were settlers (non-Indigenous) in this country and who have benefitted from legislation and policies that caused serious generational harm to Indigenous people. My family and I have also felt the generational impacts of colonization. My mom comes from the Nanapay and Cardinal family of Peepeekisis First Nation in Saskatchewan, but she didn't grow up there. She was adopted into a non-Indigenous family in rural Saskatchewan. She grow up knowing she was an Indian, the term used at that time. All you had to do was look at her beautiful brown eyes and dark skin to know she was Indigenous. But it wasn't until 1990 that we learned about our culture and traditions, and not until 2008 that we met her brothers. So my family has had its own journey of reconciliation.

My dad is of Scottish and Lakota ancestry. His side of the family knows little about this ancestry. Keep in

colonize—to send settlers to a place in order to establish political control over it. This is done by creating new governing systems and ways of living, being and doing that make the ways of those who were there before inferior. This creates unequal relationships between the colonizer and the Indigenous people.

mind, they come from a generation in which there was extreme **racism** toward Indigenous people, and as a result some of them internalized and accepted it. While my sister and I have attempted to uncover the roots of our family tree, many people who would know the answers have now passed away, and our inquiries often lead to more questions than answers. I know my experience is not unique. There are generations of people in our country with similar stories. Perhaps you even see your family in my story.

There were days when tears rolled down my cheeks as I wrote. Sometimes they were tears of awe at the humanity, empathy and hope young people like you have. Other days the tears flowed as I listened to and read the stories of Residential School Survivors and their families. It's not in my nature to ask for support, but I've learned over the years how important it is! I am immensely grateful to the family and friends who accompanied me on this journey and who were there to listen, dry my tears and encourage me to keep writing.

I hope you remember this as you read *and* go on your own journey. It's okay to ask for support and to provide support when somebody else needs it. Please take care of yourself on this journey. Listen and learn with your heart. I hope the book will inspire you. Some of it might hurt you and make you angry. That's okay. Use it as fuel to help make change in a positive way. ●

racism—discrimination and prejudice toward a person or people because of their race.

As you begin planning any trip or journey, you start by asking yourself questions. They might include:

▸ Where do I want to go, or where am I going to go?

▸ Why do I want to go there?

▸ What do I want to see, feel, experience, learn?

▸ Whom do I want to meet?

To help you answer some of those questions, let's explore what you'll find in this book.

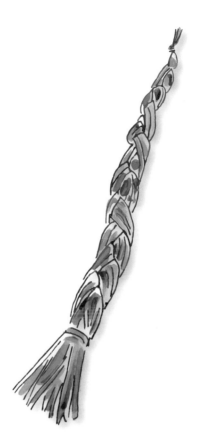

POWERFUL MEDICINE

I have designed the chapters based on a three-strand braid of sweetgrass. I've been taught by Elder Fred John from the Xaxli'p Nation that sweetgrass is one of four traditional medicines. The other three sacred medicines are sage, cedar and tobacco (not the tobacco in cigarettes, but sacred tobacco grown specifically for ceremonies).

Sweetgrass grows on the plains in swampy grassy areas, and after it is harvested, it is woven into braids. I've been taught that the three strands of the braid represent honesty, love and kindness. Sweetgrass has a beautiful sweet

A bundle of sweetgrass tied in a Métis sash.
SHIRLEY TURCOTTE

19

smell, and in some First Nations it is known as "the hair of Mother Earth." It is used for smudging, or cleansing, and also to fill a person or a space with positive energy and hopeful feelings. That is what I hope you will feel as you embark on this journey.

Smudging is a form of ceremony that involves burning medicines and bringing the smoke over your body. It is a traditional way of cleansing the four parts of yourself—your mind, body, emotions and spirit. You know how most days you have a shower or bath to clean your body? Well, smudging is just like that. The smoke from the medicine "washes over" your body. It helps clean the parts of yourself you don't see—your emotions, your spirit and your mind.

Throughout this book there are beautiful teachings I have received on my journey. They come from my relatives, Elders, Residential School Survivors and the many other people who have shared their ideas and wisdom. It is up to you to decide which things you want to put into your "backpack" and use to support you in leading a good life.

ISTOCK.COM

A Starry Night

When you look up at the night sky and see the Big Dipper, you will see seven stars…one for each of the seven Sacred Teachings.

THE SEVEN SACRED TEACHINGS

In some Nations, sweetgrass is braided using seven strands. Each strand represents one of the Seven Sacred Teachings, also known as the Grandfather Teachings. The teachings have many layers, and the right to learn the deeper layers of the teachings is earned by demonstrating you are a respectful, caring and helpful citizen. When we follow these teachings, we live in greater harmony and peace, not just in our own hearts and lives, but also in our families, schools and society as a whole. I will be sharing the first layer of the teachings with you.

Relationships are central to the Indigenous world view. Everything revolves around relationships. This is one of the reasons you may hear **Elders**, **Traditional Knowledge Keepers** and speakers say "all my relations" at the end of their sharing. It is a way of acknowledging that we are connected to all living things—not just to human beings, but to the land, the water and the animals, including those that swim, fly and crawl. The Indigenous world view is woven into our **oral traditions** and stories, our ceremonies, and our songs and dances, to name just a few examples.

Let's learn a bit about the teachings…

Elders—An Elder is often an older person who is considered wise because of their knowledge and understanding of the land, language, traditional ways, teachings, stories and ceremonies.

Traditional Knowledge Keepers—people who know, hold, protect and share traditional and local knowledge. Often traditional knowledge has been orally passed for generations, through stories, legends, rituals and songs.

oral traditions—communication whereby knowledge, ideas, stories and teachings are protected and shared verbally. Sharing may occur through conversation, storytelling or song and gets passed from one generation to another.

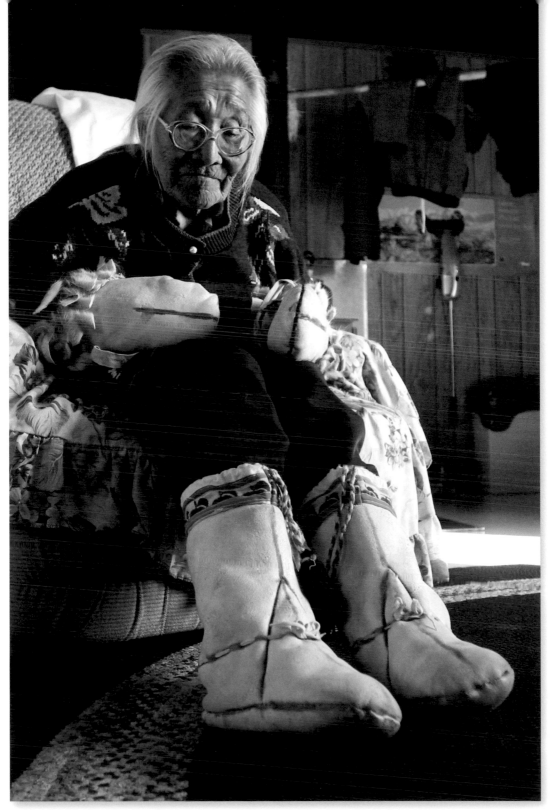

Elders have always been a source of wisdom and strength for younger generations. DEDDEDA WHITE

Honesty

Being honest with ourselves and speaking our truth is important in all aspects of our lives. A key part of this is knowing who we are and what our gifts are. Honesty also means having integrity. When you say one thing but act in a different way, this is known as being "out of integrity." Be honest in both your words and your actions.

Respect

Respect means honouring and taking care of yourself, your loved ones, the land, the water and the animals. It is about taking and using only what you need and sharing the rest. When we treat others as we would like to be treated, that is an act of respect.

Love

Love is, in many ways, what life is all about—love for ourselves, our family, our friends, our pets, our homes, the land we live on. Love, and especially love of self, is important not only in reconciliation but in all aspects of our lives.

Courage/Bravery

When we go through hard times or face challenges, we strengthen our inner muscle of courage…and no matter who we are, where we live, how old we are, where we go to school or how much money our family has, we will all need to have courage at different times in our lives.

Truth

One form of truth is being grateful for all you have in your heart and in your life, even if what is going on is painful. Sometimes the truth is uncomfortable and hurtful, but it is essential to know the truth if we are to live good lives. Truth can also be beautiful and healing.

Humility

Being humble is a dance between having healthy self-esteem and not being arrogant or thinking too highly of yourself. I encourage you to stand in your strengths and gifts and be humble. Have faith that things will work out, not always how you want them to or how you think they should, but always in your highest good.

Wisdom

There is a big difference between knowledge and wisdom. Knowledge can be learned. For example, I hope you learn a lot from reading this book. Wisdom comes from lived experiences and what we learn from those experiences. Wisdom is coming to understand the unique gifts you have been blessed with. Remember, there is no one like you on this earth, no one with the same set of gifts. Use your gifts in a positive way.

Reflections

What stood out most for you in the Seven Sacred Teachings?

›2‹

HONESTY

Where Have We Come From?

> "This is not an Aboriginal problem. This is a Canadian problem. Because at the same time that Aboriginal people were being demeaned in the schools and their culture and language were being taken away from them and they were being told that they were inferior, they were pagans, that they were heathens and savages and that they were unworthy of being respected—that very same message was being given to the non-Aboriginal children in public schools as well. They need to know that history includes them."
>
> **Justice Murray Sinclair**, *Ottawa Citizen*, May 24, 2015

◄ Three boys at Pelican Residential School near Sioux Lookout, ON.
OA C330 13-0-0-162

Until recently the honest history of Canada and Indigenous people had rarely been told. It is critical for us as a country to tell this truth and for you as a young citizen to know this history so that we can learn from it and ensure that it is never repeated.

KNOWING THE TRUTH

A key part of honesty is recognizing and accepting the truth. Some parts of this history can be hard to believe, and at times it can hurt to learn how legislation and policies have impacted the **First Peoples** of this country.

But on any journey it is critical to know where you've come from and where you are before you plan where you want to go. It's the same for our journey of reconciliation. In order to understand the need for and importance of reconciliation, we must first know the truth. In this chapter I will share with you aspects of Canadian history and policies that gave root to the Residential School system.

Sometimes people refer to this part of our country's story as Indigenous history, but in my

Cartier Meets the Indians of the St. Lawrence, 1535, by C.W.Jefferys. LAC 2835907

First Peoples—the descendants of the original people living in Canada.

mind this is Canadian history. It is not something in our past or something we are "over." It is still very much lived every day...in our homes, in our communities, on our streets and in the houses of government, both provincial and federal, where decisions and laws are made.

Colonization and **cultural genocide** unfolded at different times and in different ways for Indigenous peoples across this land, often resulting in devastating loss.

This chapter provides only a small glimpse into the truth. If you want to learn more, I encourage you to do so. There are many beautiful books— both fiction and nonfiction— written by Indigenous authors that cover this history. As well, you can watch multiple documentaries, like CBC's *8th Fire* series, and numerous YouTube videos to learn more. Please visit this book's website, www.speakingourtruth.ca, for links to videos and information on other resources.

First Nations woman and baby, 1918.
LAC 3367134

Cultural Genocide

"Cultural genocide is the destruction of those structures and practices that allow the group to continue as a group. States that engage in cultural genocide set out to destroy the political and social institutions of the targeted group. Land is seized, and populations are forcibly transferred and their movement is restricted. Languages are banned. Spiritual leaders are persecuted, spiritual practices are forbidden, and objects of spiritual value are confiscated and destroyed. And, most significantly to the issue at hand, families are disrupted to prevent the transmission of cultural values and identity from one generation to the next. In its dealing with Aboriginal people, Canada did all these things.

—*Honouring the Truth, Reconciling for the Future: Summary of the Final Report of the Truth and Reconciliation Commission of Canada*

Cree thirst dance.
UCCA 93.049P/892N

PRE-CONTACT

Pre-contact refers to the time before Europeans arrived in Canada. Indigenous people have lived on the land of what we now call Canada, since—well, let's just say for generations before we were "found" by European explorers. The name of our country—Canada—comes from the Haudenosaunee word *kanata*, which means "the village."

In the pre-contact period, each Nation had its own ceremonies, protocols and beliefs, but we shared a similar world view—a way of being, doing and living. The majority of Indigenous Nations travelled between winter and summer camps and were able to survive in harsh environments. Living off the land and water was a way of life that fostered a deep connection to and respect for the earth, the sky and all living things. Indigenous people believed and still do believe that the land is alive and vibrant, and water is medicine. Think about it—we can go a long time without eating food, but we need water in order to survive.

Indigenous people remain stewards of the land and water, and care for them and protect them in the best way possible. Traditional languages are deeply connected to the land.

The way Indigenous people hunt now, in most cases, reflects ancient traditions. Every part of the animal was used for either food, clothing, shelter or ceremony. Nothing was ever wasted, and the food hunted and gathered was shared with family and community members. Wealth was often determined by how much a person or family could give away and share with other families and community members.

In Indigenous communities across this land, it is believed that raising children is a sacred responsibility—children themselves are considered sacred. They are to be cherished and raised in the best way possible. All children are born

Look After Yourself

This chapter contains information and stories that may be upsetting for you. It is important that you take care of yourself as you read this book. Be sure to do some of these simple things.

- Drink water
- Stretch and move (if you are reading this in class, remember the teaching of respect and be sure not to disrupt others)
- Take a deep breath and focus on the exhale
- Talk with someone you trust
- Reach out to your parents, teacher, school counsellor, Elders

with a unique set of gifts, or, as some might say, talents. The Elders and family members help children develop their gifts so they can use them to contribute to the wellness of the world.

As you read this chapter, you will see how Canadian legislation and policies significantly disrupted this sacred responsibility.

The Umbrella of Indigenous Resiliency

In 2000, I created the Umbrella of Indigenous Resiliency to illustrate some of the key legislative decisions that have occurred and caused harm to Indigenous people. Take a moment to look at the Umbrella. At the top are historical events. Many stories and ripple effects accompany each of them.

I talk about some of these events on the following pages. The words that accompany the raindrops (or, as some say, the teardrops) name some of the ways this history has impacted and continues to impact Indigenous people. The handle is made up of the four "blankets" that I think foster **resiliency** in

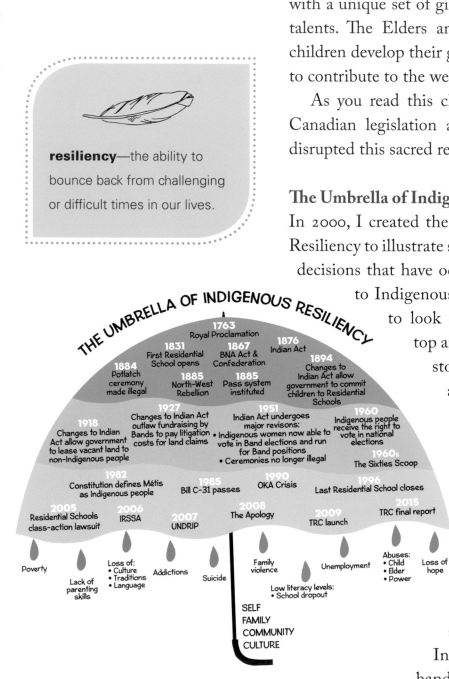

resiliency—the ability to bounce back from challenging or difficult times in our lives.

THE UMBRELLA OF INDIGENOUS RESILIENCY

1763 Royal Proclamation
1831 First Residential School opens
1867 BNA Act & Confederation
1876 Indian Act
1884 Potlatch ceremony made illegal
1885 North-West Rebellion
1885 Pass system instituted
1894 Changes to Indian Act allow government to commit children to Residential Schools
1918 Changes to Indian Act allow government to lease vacant land to non-Indigenous people
1927 Changes to Indian Act outlaw fundraising by Bands to pay litigation costs for land claims
1951 Indian Act undergoes major revisons:
• Indigenous women now able to vote in Band elections and run for Band positions
• Ceremonies no longer illegal
1960 Indigenous people receive the right to vote in national elections
1960s The Sixties Scoop
1982 Constitution defines Métis as Indigenous people
1985 Bill C-31 passes
1990 OKA Crisis
1996 Last Residential School closes
2005 Residential Schools class-action lawsuit
2006 IRSSA
2007 UNDRIP
2008 The Apology
2009 TRC launch
2015 TRC final report

Poverty
Lack of parenting skills
Loss of:
• Culture
• Traditions
• Language
Addictions
Suicide
Family violence
Low literacy levels:
• School dropout
Unemployment
Abuses:
• Child
• Elder
• Power
Loss of hope

SELF
FAMILY
COMMUNITY
CULTURE

Indigenous people. I chose to call it the Umbrella of Indigenous Resiliency because when I think about this history, I think about how extraordinarily resilient Indigenous people are. I hope that as you review the Umbrella and the rest of the information in this chapter, you will begin to see that resilience.

THE HISTORICAL JOURNEY

So...where do we begin? How about over in Britain? I know, I know. Britain seems like a peculiar starting point when we are talking about Canadian history, but let me explain. In 1763, after Britain won the Seven Years' War, King George III issued the Royal Proclamation and officially claimed territory for Britain in North America. The British realized that positive and respectful relationships with the **Indians** would be integral to the future of the colonies. As part of honouring the relationship, the Royal Proclamation clearly stated that all land would be considered Indian land until ceded by Treaty.

Treaties

In 1867 the British North America Act made Indian education a federal government responsibility. Also in 1867, **Confederation** occurred, Canada became a country, and the Treaty-making process began. The Treaties set out obligations,

Indians—a term used to describe the First Peoples of Canada up until the 1980s.

Confederation—the process by which the British Colonies of Canada, Nova Scotia and New Brunswick were united into one Dominion of Canada on July 1, 1867. Eventually the other provinces and territories joined and created what we know as Canada today.

Indian Act—the body of Canadian laws that sets out federal government responsibilities for managing reserve lands, money and other resources. It was first passed in 1876 and has been altered several times since then.

benefits and promises for both Canada and the First Nations signing the Treaties. A vast portion of Canada is covered by Treaties.

Each Treaty included a promise that the government would provide education. Initially, this came in the form of Indian day schools, which were located in or near First Nation communities and were different from Residential Schools in that students returned home at the end of the school day. But like Residential Schools, day schools were funded by the federal or provincial governments and run by the churches, and the same abuses occurred in them as in the Residential Schools. Their overall message was that traditional Indigenous ways of being were inferior to non-Indigenous ways. All of this contributed to shame and the loss of language, culture and pride.

Royal Proclamation issued by King George III in 1763.
CLEMENTS LIBRARY, UNIVERSITY OF MICHIGAN

The Indian Act

In 1876 the **Indian Act** became law and legally distinguished between First Nations and other Canadians. While it acknowledged the federal government had a unique relationship with, and obligation to, First Nations, the purpose of the Indian Act

> **"In some locations, Canada negotiated Treaties with First Nations; in others, the land was simply occupied or seized. The negotiation of Treaties, while seemingly honourable and legal, was often marked by fraud and coercion."**
> **Truth and Reconciliation Commission**, Summary of the Final Report

was **assimilation**. The Indian Act is still in place today, but it has undergone a number of changes over the years.

As part of the initial Indian Act, Chieftainships and traditional systems of governance were abolished, and elected Band Councils were implemented. Keep in mind that at this time in Canadian history, women were not yet considered persons, so they couldn't vote or run for any Band Council positions. This was a significant disruption to traditional ways of doing business, especially in the Nations that were **matriarchal** and **matrilineal**—where the women were the leaders.

The Indian Act defined who qualified as an Indian and who was eligible for **Indian status**. This legislation determined status through the male line. For example, if an Indian woman married a non-Indian man (whether non-Indian or non-status), she lost her status and her right to live on her reserve and access Treaty and other benefits. If she married an Indian man from another band, she would have

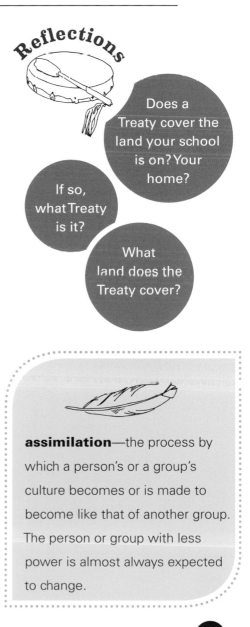

Reflections

Does a Treaty cover the land your school is on? Your home?

If so, what Treaty is it?

What land does the Treaty cover?

assimilation—the process by which a person's or a group's culture becomes or is made to become like that of another group. The person or group with less power is almost always expected to change.

matriarchal—describes a society in which the positions of power or respect are held by women, and women are highly regarded.

~~~~~

matrilineal—tracing family relationships through the female line, rather than the male line, meaning that children would inherit from their mother's side, not their father's.

~~~~~

Indian status—a person's legal status as an Indian, as defined by the Indian Act.

~~~~~

Potlatch—a ceremonial feast acknowledging important events such as births, deaths, marriages, etc. Gift-giving and honouring of guests are integral aspects of the ceremony. Potlatch is not part of every First Nation's culture.

to become a member of her husband's band to have status. Legally, her status was conditional on her husband's status.

In 1884 the federal government implemented legislation that made the **Potlatch** ceremony illegal. Changes in later years also made the Sun Dance illegal.

For a number of reasons, 1885 was a significant year in history. First, the North-West Rebellion, led by **Métis** leader Louis Riel, occurred. (Some Métis people are offended by the term *rebellion* and prefer to call it a *resistance*.)

The Métis believed that Canada had failed to protect their rights, their land and their survival as a distinct people. The rebellion ended when the Métis were defeated at Batoche. Riel was captured and later convicted of treason, and despite many pleas from across Canada for amnesty, he was hanged.

Also in 1885, the Department of Indian Affairs instituted the "pass system." This meant that no Indigenous person could leave the reserve without a pass from the

Métis leader Louis Riel was tried for treason and executed on November 16, 1885.
LAC 3228116

Department of Indian Affairs

.... Duck Lake .... Agency.

.... Nov 1st 1932

Edward Yahyahkeekoot. No. 125

of .... Beardy's ....

.... Band

is permitted to be absent from his Reserve for *Two weeks*

days from date hereof. Business *Trapping in ....*

hunting for food and is .... permitted to carry a gun.

....
Indian Agent.

A pass provided to Mr. Yahyahkeekoot to leave Beardy's First Nation. SASKATCHEWAN ARCHIVES

Indian agent, and no one could come onto the reserve to do business without a pass.

In 1894 a change to the Indian Act made it mandatory for Indian children between the ages of seven and sixteen to attend Residential School. It was changed again in 1908 to apply to children between six and fifteen years of age. It was this law that allowed RCMP to arrest parents if they did not surrender their children to go to Residential School. Mandatory attendance was in effect until 1948. Even after that, for a variety of reasons, many Indian children continued to go to Residential Schools.

In 1927 the Indian Act prohibited Indians from raising money to hire legal counsel to fight for land claims. This shut down the capacity of Indians to pursue land claims and remained in effect until 1951.

Métis—people of First Nation and European ancestry who identify as being Métis and can link their heritage to the historic Red River settlement. The term has different historical and contemporary meanings, however, and is sometimes used to describe anyone of European-First Nation ancestry who identifies as Métis. Métis ancestors are most often Scottish, French, Ojibwe and Cree.

Children dance at a Pow Wow in Ohsweken, ON. PETERKBURIAN.COM.

> **"The great aim of our legislation has been to do away with the tribal system and assimilate the Indian people in all respects."**
>
> **Sir John A. Macdonald**,
> prime minister of Canada, 1887

In 1951 the Indian Act underwent major revisions. Women were now allowed to vote in and run for Band elections. As well, ceremonies were no longer illegal, and Indigenous people could wear regalia without the permission of an Indian agent.

Although women received the right to vote in Band elections in 1951, Indigenous people didn't receive the right to vote in national elections until 1960.

The Sixties Scoop

The Sixties Scoop refers to a period in the 1960s when Indigenous children were removed from their families by child-welfare authorities who deemed the children's parents unfit to raise them. In most cases, children were removed without the consent of their families or Bands.

> **"The education of Indians consists not merely of training the mind but of a weaning from the habits and feelings of their ancestors and the acquirements of the language, arts and customs of civilized life."**
>
> **Egerton Ryerson**, chief superintendent of education in Upper Canada, 1847 report to Department of Indian Affairs

Many of the children who were taken from their families as part of the Sixties Scoop were adopted far from their home communities, by families who did not know the importance of Indigenous culture, language and connection to ancestral land. While some children were placed in loving homes, others were abused by their foster or adoptive families. Anxiety and culture shock were common. Children often had difficulty developing attachments and felt they did not belong in either mainstream or Indigenous society. Parents who lost their children had feelings of powerlessness, grief and helplessness and often turned to unhealthy coping behaviours to numb the pain of their loss.

On February 14, 2017, an Ontario court judge ruled in favour of the Survivors in a class-action lawsuit linked to the Sixties Scoop. The ruling acknowledges that Canada failed to take reasonable steps to prevent children from losing their connection to their language, culture and identity.

The ruling states, "Neither the children nor their foster or adoptive parents were given

Reflections

Why do you think the Government of Canada made it illegal for Indigenous people to practise their ceremonies?

How do you think Indigenous people kept ceremonies alive from 1884 to 1951?

Have you seen any revitalization of culture and ceremonies in the territory where you live?

> **"This provision of the Indian Act was in place for close to 75 years and what that did was it prevented the passing down of our oral history. It prevented the passing down of our values. It meant an interruption of the respected forms of government that we used to have, and we did have forms of government be they oral and not in writing before any of the Europeans came to this country. We had a system that worked for us. We respected each other. We had ways of dealing with disputes."**
>
> **Judge Alfred Scow**, Royal Commission on Aboriginal Peoples

information about the children's aboriginal heritage or about the various educational and other benefits that they were entitled to receive."

While this ruling is specific to children apprehended from families in Ontario, it is precedent-setting for all the other provinces and territories.

Legal Changes

In 1982 changes to Canada's constitution became law and included the recognition of Indian, **Inuit** and Métis as Aboriginal peoples with existing rights. In 1985 the federal government passed Bill C-31 to bring the rules about status in the Indian Act in line with the rules about gender equality under the Charter of Rights and Freedoms. Status was to be reinstated to women and their children who had lost it through the previous discriminatory legislation.

On September 13, 2007, the United Nations Declaration on the Rights of Indigenous Peoples

Inuit—the word means "people" in Inuktitut (the Inuit language). In Canada, the word describes the First People who live in Nunavut, Northwest Territories and northern Quebec and Labrador.

The First Female Chief

Elsie Marie Knott was the first woman in Canada to be elected chief of a First Nation. She was elected chief of the Curve Lake First Nation in 1954, three years after the Indian Act was amended to give First Nations women the right to vote and hold positions in Band governments.

(UNDRIP) was formally adopted by the General Assembly. A majority of 143 countries voted in favour, while four countries voted against it: Australia, Canada, New Zealand and the United States. It took almost a decade—until May 2016—and a newly elected Liberal government to remove Canada's objector status to the UN Declaration on the Rights of Indigenous Peoples.

THE RESIDENTIAL SCHOOLS

Survivors Speak

We owe a great debt of gratitude to the Survivors of Residential Schools and their families. It's through their courage and resilience and sharing of experiences that we are afforded a glimpse into what life was like before, during and after Residential School. *Kinanâskomitin!* Thank you!

Unless otherwise noted, the stories that follow are from *The Survivors Speak: A Report of the Truth and Reconciliation Commission of Canada*, released in 2015. In their preface to the report, the commissioners share what it means to be a survivor:

Kids in "Care"

The Sixties Scoop continued the cycle of family breakdown. Today there are three times as many First Nations children in the government's care than there were at the height of the Residential School system.

—First Nations Child & Family Caring Society of Canada

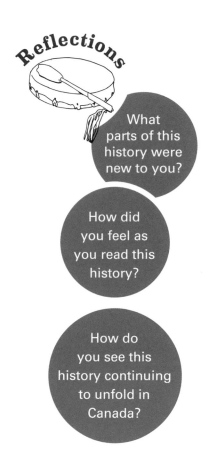

Reflections

What parts of this history were new to you?

How did you feel as you read this history?

How do you see this history continuing to unfold in Canada?

"A Survivor is not just someone who 'made it through' the schools, or 'got by' or was 'making do.' A Survivor is a person who persevered against and overcame adversity…It referred to someone who had taken all that could be thrown at them and remained standing at the end. It came to mean someone who could legitimately say 'I am still here!' For that achievement, Survivors deserve our highest respect. But, for that achievement, we also owe them the debt of doing the right thing. Reconciliation is the right thing to do, coming out of this history."

Life Before Residential School

Since time immemorial, Indigenous ways of living, doing and being, including cultural and spiritual practices, values and beliefs, have been passed along from one generation to the next. In many communities, this included children being raised with grandparents, on the land and immersed in their language and traditional way of living. One of the responsibilities of aunties, uncles and grandparents, as well as the community, was to watch children to see what gift(s) they had been born with, and then help them strengthen and use those gifts in service of their family, community and Nation.

The following story provides us with a glimpse of what life was like for one Indigenous boy before he was sent to Residential School.

Noel's Journey

Noel Starblanket was in Residential School for eleven years and went on to become the chief of Star Blanket Cree Nation at the age of twenty-four. He later became the president of the National Indian Brotherhood (now known as the Assembly of First Nations). Noel recounts in *The Survivors Speak* that, prior to Residential School, "I attended ceremonies, I went to Sun Dances. I picked medicines with them. We did medicine ceremonies. We did pipe ceremonies. We did feasts. We did all of those things with my grandparents, and I spent time with my grandfather in those ceremonies, and I worked with my grandfather. He made me work at a very tender age. I was cutting wood, cutting pickets, cutting hay, hauling hay, all of that kind of stuff, looking after animals, horses and cattle. So, I spent a lot of good times with my grandparents, my…and the love that I had from them, and the kindness, and the very deep spirituality that they had. And so my formative years were with them. I would spend time with my parents, but not a whole lot. So, mostly my grandparents raised me. My parents never hit me, my grandparents. I didn't know what, what it meant to be hit, physically abused. All I needed was one stare, or one look from my dad, or my grandfather, and my grandmother or my mother would always say '*wâpam awa*' [look at that one], then I would stop what I was doing, because I knew how to respect my grandfather and my dad, didn't have to hit us,

Photo: University of Regina Photography Dept.

Reflections

How would you feel if the RCMP showed up at your house and took you away to a school far from your home?

Why do you think children were still attending the schools until 1996?

just, just took one look. And so I grew up with that. And if we were acting foolish, or anything like that, or misbehaving, or whatever, they would just tell us in a good, kind way not to behave like that, and or if we were acting too silly, or whatever, they would tell us to calm down. They would always tell us that if you're gonna hit a high like that, you're gonna hit low, and I'll always remember that teaching, 'cause I tell my grandchildren the same thing." ●

The Lifespan of Residential Schools

There is a myth in Canada that Residential Schools existed a long time ago. While most of the schools had closed by the mid-1970s, the last federally run Residential School, Gordon's School in Punnichy, Saskatchewan, closed in 1996.

The first recognized Residential School was the Mohawk Institute in Brantford, Ontario. It opened in 1831 and operated until 1962. Over 130 schools operated over the years. These schools served over 150,000 First Nations, Métis and Inuit children.

Let's think about this for a moment, about the impact of Residential Schools being open *for 165 years*. When you think of this in terms of families, it means seven generations of families could have gone to the schools.

The Mohawk Institute in Brantford, ON, was the first Residential School in Canada. THE GENERAL SYNOD ARCHIVES, ANGLICAN CHURCH OF CANADA

> ## "The Residential School experience established for Canada's Indigenous population is one of the darkest, most troubling chapters in our nation's history."
>
> **Justice Murray Sinclair**, TRC Final Report, Volume 1

Bringing It Close to Home...

Take a look at the map of Residential Schools on the next pages and figure out which school was closest to where you live.

Daily Life

Academic studies took a back seat to religious instruction at Residential Schools, and the development of job-related skills all too often meant that boys were responsible for the livestock and fieldwork, while girls cleaned the school, worked in the kitchen and sewed and washed clothes.

Writing about what Residential School Survivors and their families experienced was exceptionally difficult for me, for a couple of reasons. First, I had the difficult task of deciding which stories to include and which to leave out. Doing this without being disrespectful of the Survivors' stories and lived experiences was, without question, the greatest challenge of writing this book! Second, it was deeply painful for me, especially as a mom, to read so many stories of abuse and harm of children.

Boys learn carpentry skills at Brandon Indian Industrial School, ca 1910. UCCA 93.049P/1368N

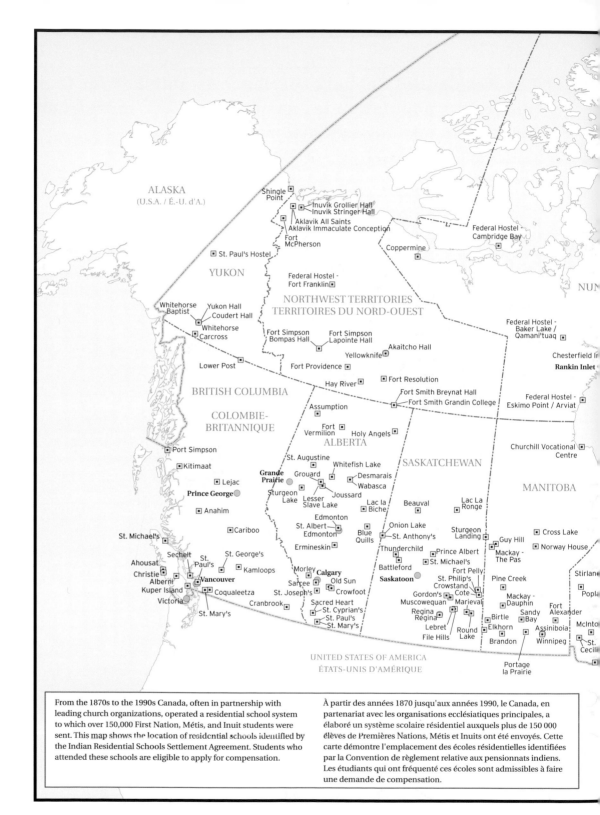

ALASKA
(U.S.A. / É.-U. d'A.)

Shingle Point

Inuvik Grollier Hall
Inuvik Stringer Hall
Aklavik All Saints
Aklavik Immaculate Conception
Fort McPherson

Coppermine

Federal Hostel - Cambridge Bay

St. Paul's Hostel

YUKON

Federal Hostel - Fort Franklin

NORTHWEST TERRITORIES
TERRITOIRES DU NORD-OUEST

NUN

Whitehorse Baptist
Yukon Hall
Coudert Hall
Whitehorse
Carcross

Fort Simpson Bompas Hall
Fort Simpson Lapointe Hall
Akaitcho Hall
Yellowknife

Federal Hostel - Baker Lake / Qamani'tuaq

Chesterfield I

Lower Post

Fort Providence

Hay River

Fort Resolution

Rankin Inlet

BRITISH COLUMBIA

Assumption

Fort Smith Breynat Hall
Fort Smith Grandin College

Federal Hostel - Eskimo Point / Arviat

COLOMBIE-BRITANNIQUE

Fort Vermilion
Holy Angels

ALBERTA

Churchill Vocational Centre

Port Simpson

St. Augustine

Whitefish Lake

SASKATCHEWAN

Kitimaat

Grande Prairie
Grouard
Desmarais
Wabasca

MANITOBA

Lejac

Sturgeon Lake
Lesser Slave Lake
Joussard

Prince George

Anahim

Lac la Biche
Beauval
Lac La Ronge

Cross Lake

Cariboo

Edmonton
St. Albert
Edmonton
Blue Quills
Onion Lake
St. Anthony's
Sturgeon Landing
Guy Hill
Norway House

St. Michael's

Ermineskin

Thunderchild
Prince Albert
Mackay - The Pas

Ahousat
Christie
Alberni
Kuper Island
Victoria

Sechelt
St. Paul's
St. George's
Kamloops
Vancouver
Coqualeetza

Morley
Sarcee
Calgary
Old Sun
St. Joseph's
Crowfoot

Battleford
St. Michael's
Fort Pelly
St. Philip's
Crowstand
Cote

Stirlan

Pine Creek

Cranbrook

Sacred Heart
St. Cyprian's
St. Paul's
St. Mary's

Gordon's
Muscowequan
Marieval
Mackay - Dauphin
Fort Alexander

Poph

St. Mary's

Regina
Regina
Lebret
File Hills
Round Lake
Birtle
Sandy Bay
Elkhorn
Assiniboia
Brandon
Winnipeg

McInto

St. Cecili

UNITED STATES OF AMERICA
ÉTATS-UNIS D'AMÉRIQUE

Portage la Prairie

From the 1870s to the 1990s Canada, often in partnership with leading church organizations, operated a residential school system to which over 150,000 First Nation, Métis, and Inuit students were sent. This map shows the location of residential schools identified by the Indian Residential Schools Settlement Agreement. Students who attended these schools are eligible to apply for compensation.

À partir des années 1870 jusqu'aux années 1990, le Canada, en partenariat avec les organisations ecclésiatiques principales, a élaboré un système scolaire résidentiel auxquels plus de 150 000 élèves de Premières Nations, Métis et Inuits ont été envoyés. Cette carte démontre l'emplacement des écoles résidentielles identifiées par la Convention de règlement relative aux pensionnats indiens. Les étudiants qui ont fréquenté ces écoles sont admissibles à faire une demande de compensation.

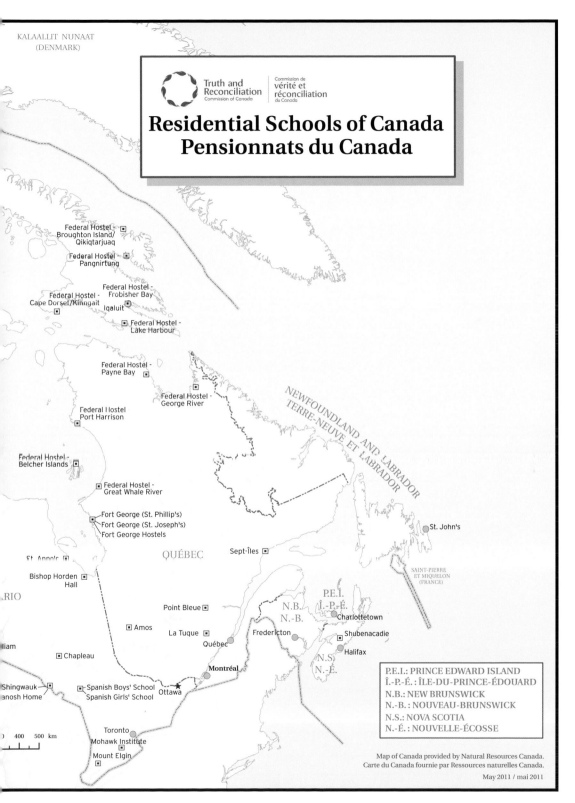

KALAALLIT NUNAAT
(DENMARK)

Residential Schools of Canada
Pensionnats du Canada

Truth and Reconciliation Commission of Canada

Commission de vérité et réconciliation du Canada

Federal Hostel - Broughton Island/ Qikiqtarjuaq

Federal Hostel - Pangnirtung

Federal Hostel - Cape Dorset/Kinngait

Federal Hostel - Frobisher Bay

Iqaluit

Federal Hostel - Lake Harbour

Federal Hostel - Payne Bay

Federal Hostel - George River

Federal Hostel Port Harrison

NEWFOUNDLAND AND LABRADOR
TERRE-NEUVE ET LABRADOR

Federal Hostel - Belcher Islands

Federal Hostel - Great Whale River

Fort George (St. Phillip's)
Fort George (St. Joseph's)
Fort George Hostels

St. John's

QUÉBEC

Sept-Îles

SAINT-PIERRE ET MIQUELON (FRANCE)

Bishop Horden Hall

Point Bleue

P.E.I.
Î.-P.-É.

N.B.
N.-B.

Charlottetown

RIO

Amos

La Tuque

Fredericton

Shubenacadie

Chapleau

Québec

Halifax

N.S.
N.-É.

Montréal

liam

Shingwauk
anosh Home

Spanish Boys' School
Spanish Girls' School

Ottawa

P.E.I.: PRINCE EDWARD ISLAND
Î.-P.-É.: ÎLE-DU-PRINCE-ÉDOUARD
N.B.: NEW BRUNSWICK
N.-B.: NOUVEAU-BRUNSWICK
N.S.: NOVA SCOTIA
N.-É.: NOUVELLE-ÉCOSSE

400   500 km

Toronto
Mohawk Institute
Mount Elgin

Map of Canada provided by Natural Resources Canada.
Carte du Canada fournie par Ressources naturelles Canada.

May 2011 / mai 2011

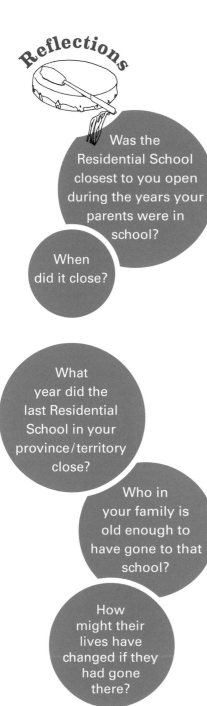

Reflections

Was the Residential School closest to you open during the years your parents were in school?

When did it close?

What year did the last Residential School in your province/territory close?

Who in your family is old enough to have gone to that school?

How might their lives have changed if they had gone there?

Positive Experiences: The Uncommon Voices

As with all things in life, not everyone who shares the same experience feels the same way about it *or* remembers it the same way. While the majority of Residential School Survivors describe their time at school as full of fear, loneliness, hunger and abuse, some students talk about the positive impact of education, sports, learning English and developing a strong work ethic.

The first time I heard anyone speak positively about Residential School was in 1991. I was working as an alcohol and drug counsellor in a small community in the interior of British Columbia, and I often visited with the Elders. During one of these visits an Elder said to me, "You must understand that there are always two sides to everything. For me, Residential School was a positive experience. We need to be open to hearing from those of us who had a good experience there." She shared this with me during a time when many former students were coming forward with their stories of abuse and trauma, and I remember thinking how courageous she was to share a different perspective.

The second time I heard a similar message was in 1999. I was in Yellowknife, facilitating trauma training sessions for counsellors working with Residential School Survivors. The counsellors came from across the Northwest Territories, and the majority of them were former students themselves. We were having a sharing circle, and it was full of heavy emotions as the eagle feather went around and each person had a chance to share. Near the end of the circle it came to a woman from Old Crow, who sat stroking that feather for a long time. No words, just stroking the feather. After a bit she inhaled deeply and began to share. "I know many of you ain't gonna believe me and some of you will be real mad at me for sayin' this, but —" She paused and took another deep breath before she resumed. "But for me Residential School was good. I liked it there. I learned a lot I would've never learned at home, and these awful things you are all talkin' about— I didn't experience that."

Indeed, for some students, leaving home was a welcome escape. This was especially true for children whose parents had gone to Residential School and had experienced abuse and not learned positive parenting skills or strategies. These children now found themselves living in a family atmosphere that reflected the trauma their parents had experienced at Residential School.

For example, Jeanne Rioux found the Edmonton school to be a respite from an unpleasant family situation. "My mother didn't really seem to know how to show affection physically at all so there's a kind of cold atmosphere and my father was absent a lot and he was working. I was sent to boarding school

"Seven generations of Aboriginal children were denied their identity. We heard how, separated from their language, their culture and their spiritual traditions and their collective history, children became unable to answer questions as simple as: Where do I come from? Where am I going? Why am I here? And who am I?"
Justice Murray Sinclair, TRC closing ceremonies, June 2015

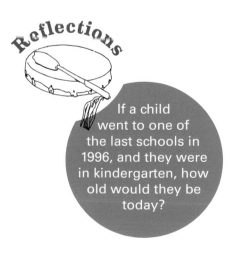

Reflections

If a child went to one of the last schools in 1996, and they were in kindergarten, how old would they be today?

The words on the blackboard read *Thou Shalt Not Tell Lies*. LAC PA134110

Protesters speak out on against the loss of Indigenous languages. FRED CATTROLL

when I was fourteen. There were a lot of people in the school that were trying to run away constantly, but I was happy to be there because it was less hurting and less anger."

Loss of Culture and Language

There is no separation between culture and language. Culture is language, and language is culture. The shame of losing either of these can be traumatizing for a child and can influence future generations.

Children were forbidden from speaking their own language and following Indigenous teachings and customs. Breaking this rule often resulted in physical discipline. Discipline was severe and abusive. These policies not only caused the significant loss of traditional languages in Indigenous families and communities, but also fostered internalized racism and lack of pride and honour in being an Indigenous person.

The Number System

The Department of Indian Affairs (part of the federal government) needed some way to keep track of students, so it created a number system. When a child arrived at Residential School, he or she was assigned a number. In many schools, these numbers were used instead of names. Marlene Kayseas shares how she never forgot the number she was given at the Lestock school in Saskatchewan. "I remember when I first went, my number was 86. I was a little small girl and I was in a small girls' dorm. And you had to remember your number because if they called you, they wouldn't call you by your name, they'd call you by your number."

Health and Wellness

Illness was a common result of high numbers of children living in small, cold, overcrowded dormitories. One of the most common illnesses in the schools was the lung disease tuberculosis (TB). When students contracted TB, they were sent to what was known as either the TB hospital or Indian hospital, where they were often

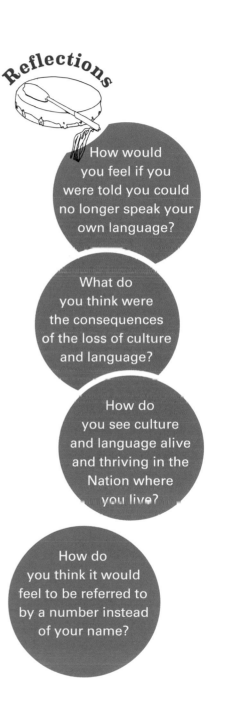

Reflections

How would you feel if you were told you could no longer speak your own language?

What do you think were the consequences of the loss of culture and language?

How do you see culture and language alive and thriving in the Nation where you live?

How do you think it would feel to be referred to by a number instead of your name?

Thomas Moore, before and after attending Residential School in Regina, SK. LAC NL022474

Students eat in the dining hall at Coppermine (Kugluktuk) school in NWT (now Nunavut), 1958. LAC 3614181

Boys ate separately from girls in the Brandon Residential School in Brandon, MB, ca 1900. UCCA 93.049P/202S

A young Frances Fletcher darns socks in the sewing room of the Anglican-run St. John's Residential School during the 1940s.
GENERAL SYNOD ARCHIVES, ANGLICAN CHURCH OF CANADA

Boys worked in the fields in many Residential Schools, while the girls worked indoors. UCCA 93.049P/1364

Sewing class at a Residential School in Resolution, NWT. LAC 3381193

Children gather for flag-raising at Round Lake Residential School, Whitewood, SK, ca 1940. UCCA 93.049P/1158

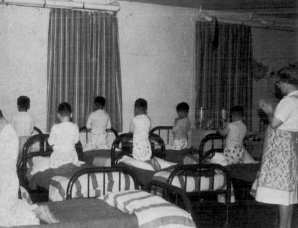

A nurse checks a girl's throat while other children wait in line in the Frobisher Bay (Iqaluit) Federal Hostel, 1959. LAC 3603557

Boys pray in their dormitory at a Residential School in the Yukon. YUKON ARCHIVES 86/61, #678

Girls in Chilliwack in 1910 work in the laundry of their Residential School. UCCA 93.049P/418N

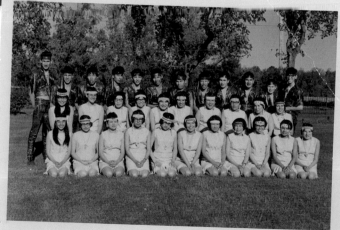

The Portage La Prairie Residential School choir, dressed as "Indians" in 1967. UCCA 93.049P/1756

> **"When the school is on the reserve, the child lives with its parents who are savages, and though he may learn to read and write, his habits and training and mode of thought are Indian. He is simply a savage who can read and write... Indian children should be withdrawn as much as possible from the parental influence, and the only way to do that would be to put them in central training industrial schools where they will acquire the habits and modes of thought of white men."**
> **Prime Minister Sir John A. Macdonald**, House of Commons, Debates, May 9, 1883

confined to their beds with no fresh air or healthy foods. They often experienced severe loneliness.

Shirley Waskewitch was at Onion Lake school and had a contagious lung illness. She was put in isolation. "Being locked up in the infirmary was one thing I never, never forget. The isolation, I, I remember that, being locked up in that room all the time. Created, created a silent fear to be in there, nothingness, nobody to talk to, just, just to lie on the bed. It used to be so quiet, and I don't know what I did to myself, just lie there on the bed, that's it, had nothing in there."

Illness was also food related. Children never had enough to eat, and what they did have was not healthy and nutritious. The constant state of hunger and the poor quality of the food led to malnutrition. Survivors who came forward during the TRC hearings often spoke of how hungry they had been and also of their efforts to secretly improve their diet. Dorothy Nolie thought it a lucky day when she was told to cut bread in the kitchen in the Alert Bay school. "We'd eat it while we're cutting it, so that was good for a while. We were cutting bread for a long time, and kids would come to me and ask me for bread, and I'd sneak it to them, 'cause I know they were hungry, too."

Recent research has revealed that nutritional experiments were conducted in at least six

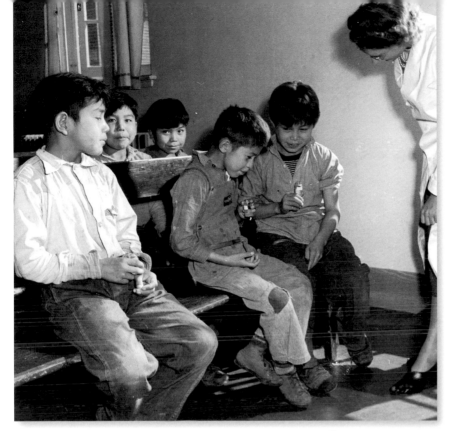

A nurse takes saliva samples from boys in Port Alberni, BC, 1948. LAC E0025046450

Residential Schools. Some students were fed lard and a clear broth soup, while others were given bread and other items that had been baked with flour mixtures full of vitamins. Parents, students and, in some cases, school staff were unaware that young people were being used this way. Research is ongoing to determine the reasons for the experiments.

The wellness of students was also impacted by the inadequate clothing they were forced to wear. It was often uncomfortable, ill-fitting and insufficient in the winter. Elaine Durocher shares what happened on her very first day at the Roman Catholic school in Kamsack, Saskatchewan.

Blood samples are taken from a child in Port Alberni, BC, 1948. LAC E002504649

> **"The federal government never established an adequate set of standards and regulations to guarantee the health and safety of Residential School students."**
>
> **Truth and Reconciliation Commission Final Report, Volume 4**

Students at the Red Deer Industrial Institute practice penmanship, ca 1914.
UCCA 93.049P/850N

"As soon as we entered the Residential School, the abuse started right away. We were stripped, taken up to a dormitory, stripped. Our hair was sprayed... They put oxfords on our feet, 'cause I know my feet hurt. They put dresses on us. And were made, we were always praying, we were always on our knees. We were told we were little, stupid savages, and that they had to educate us."

Schools were operating on meagre budgets, and the wellness of students was not a high priority. The lack of proper medical and dental care left both physical and emotional scars on students. Lydia Ross remembers that dental care at the school in Cross Lake, Manitoba, was limited and painful. "There was no anaesthesia. There was no tools like the dentist tools. They used ordinary pliers. He use, he used to be the one to pull the teeth. He used the pliers, and pulled my tooth, just put Kleenex in there or something, and there's no pain pill, you have to suffer, but I got over it, anyway."

Chastity's Journey

Chastity Davis is from the Tla'amin Nation. She is an intergenerational Residential School Survivor, an Indigenous women's advocate and a business owner/entrepreneur. Chastity didn't find out about her mom's Residential School experience until she was in her early twenties.

"My mom called me when I was at work. I will never forget what she said: 'I'm going to court in Vancouver, and I'd like you to come and support me.' I said yes and when I asked why she told me she was going to court against the government for putting all the Native kids in those schools. At that time, I didn't know what she was talking about."

Chastity describes how she sat in the courtroom hearing her mom's Residential School story for the first time: "My mom was part of the nutrition research that was being done on the kids and in hospital. Today she has lots of health problems; there's always something going on for her, including diabetes. At Residential School, they pulled out all of her teeth with minimal anaesthetic. The priests and nuns sexually abused her, and she had been physically abused too.

"I remember sitting there and being angry, really angry. The woman from the federal government who was interviewing my mom was patronizing. She was so mean to my mom, and was talking to her like she was a stupid Indian. I couldn't stand it anymore. I stood up and I lost it and told her she can't speak to

Photo: Ashley Drody

57

my mom like that. My mom's lawyer took a break then and we went outside. I was really angry with him too, for not protecting my mom."

After that, Chastity started working in First Nations communities. She has been in over 150 communities and heard the stories of Residential School Survivors. She considers it a sacred privilege to hear those stories.

Though Chastity has had the honour of hearing hundreds of stories, it doesn't heal the wounds caused by her personal ties to Residential School trauma. "A lot of what happened in my childhood and around my mom and how she showed up in the world was confusing for me." Even as a child, Chastity had a sense that something bad had happened to her mother. "She was this beautiful woman, and that is innately who she is, but how she showed up with her addictions definitely impacted me as a child." Chastity felt that she missed out on fully having the presence of a nurturing and caring mother. "I was raised with my dad and always felt this void inside of me. I grew up as a girl without a mom or female influence. That left me, as a child, never feeling good enough."

Working together is where Chastity sees a valuable future, and that future needs allies. For Chastity, an ally is somebody who feels "internally pulled, who wants to create a better future for all Canadians, not just Indigenous people. An ally is someone who has an authentic feeling of wanting to contribute to a better world." ●

These girls in Cross Lake, MB, 1940, were taught separately from the boys. LAC 4673099

Abuse: Physical, Sexual, Emotional, Psychological and Spiritual

The majority of students left Residential School with stories of fear, loneliness, hunger, harsh discipline and sexual abuse. They carried physical and emotional scars that affected their adult lives. They have had difficulty sleeping, suffered from nightmares and developed mental illnesses. Many Survivors experience low self-esteem and feel disconnected from family and community. Survivors struggle with violence, anger, guilt, addictions and other destructive patterns of behaviour.

Jean Pierre Bellemare, who attended the Amos, Québec, school, said he had been subjected to "physical violence, verbal violence, touchings, everything that comes with it."

While the statistics do not mention emotional, psychological or spiritual abuse specifically,

Nuns and students outside a school in the Yukon. LAC PA123707

these abuses were present throughout the years the Residential Schools operated. Emotional and mental abuse can take many forms and is often used as a way to control another person. It can leave "hidden scars."

Children were told never to talk about what was happening to them. Threats were used to keep them quiet. They were told God was going to punish them or their family if they said anything, or that Jesus would be angry.

Just recently it's become public that two severely abusive actions occurred at some Residential Schools: the **sterilization** of students and the use of electric chairs. What you are about to read might be very difficult to take in, and you may find yourself wondering how this could have been done to children.

In 1928, Alberta passed the Sexual Sterilization Act, which gave power to residential

sterilization—to eliminate a person's ability to have children by changing or removing his or her reproductive organs.

A Chief's Truth

Edmund Metatawabin is a former chief of Fort Albany First Nation, a writer and a former student of St. Anne's Residential School, which he attended from 1956 to 1964. His 2014 memoir *Up Ghost River: A Chief's Journey Through the Turbulent Waters of Native History* was shortlisted for a 2014 Governor General's Award.

In his statement to the TRC, Metatawabin shared how he and other students at the Fort Albany school were punished by being placed in an electric chair. It was initially constructed by the school's electrician as "an entertainment" but came to be used as a form of punishment. According to Metatawabin, it was a metal-framed chair with a wooden seat and back. After the child was buckled into the chair, an electric current from a hand-cranked generator would run through the child's body. He "sat on the electric chair three times."

school principals to have students sterilized. At least 3,500 female students were impacted by this law, which resulted in their being unable to have children. A similar act was passed in British Columbia in 1933, and it is unknown how many students were impacted, both girls and boys.

In 1996, a *Globe and Mail* article titled "Schools' electric chair haunts natives" quoted Mary Ann Nakogene Davis, who described how the electric chair at St. Anne's Residential School in Fort Albany, Ontario, was used as punishment. "They would put children in it if they were bad. The nuns used it as a weapon."

Photo: Edmund Metatawabin

Chanie Wenjack. Photo courtesy of Pearl Achneepineskum

THE CHILDREN WHO NEVER CAME HOME

In its six years of listening to more than 6,750 interviews, the TRC identified at least 3,200 confirmed deaths of children attending Residential Schools. In *The Missing Children and Unmarked Burials*, volume four of its final report, the TRC notes that deaths were primarily a result of illness.

Running away from the school was common among students who wanted to escape the abuse. Few made it home. Many were found by the school staff or RCMP, and some died in their attempt to escape the school and go home. In 1937, rare media attention was paid to Residential Schools when four boys—two aged eight and two aged nine—were found frozen together on Fraser Lake, barely a kilometre from home.

In 2016 more awareness was drawn to the children who never made it home. One of the stories garnering attention is about Chanie Wenjack, who died in 1966 while trying to get home. His tragic story inspired a music album and graphic novel called *The Secret Path*, a joint project by Gord Downie (lead singer of the Tragically Hip) and Jeff Lemire.

EFFECTS ON FAMILIES

Without question, one of the most devastating impacts of Residential Schools was—and is— the toll it took on families. Children were sent to schools far from home as a way to sever family ties. Even if there was a school in the child's community, it was common practice to send children from that community to a school somewhere else in the province or territory. Contact between children and their parents was usually discouraged, if not forbidden.

Generations of Residential School Survivors were separated by gender, in their classes, chores and sleeping dorms. In many situations, siblings and cousins were separated and sent to different schools. This conflicts directly with Indigenous traditional ways of learning through relationships and does not acknowledge the importance of the older ones taking care of the little ones. Fred John, who is from the Xaxli'p Band near Lillooet, British Columbia, talks about the profound impact this policy had on him and his sister.

"Against our will, my sister Evelyn and I were removed from our home to attend Residential School at St. Mary's in Mission, BC. I was not quite five years old and my sister was seven.

First Nations camp, Fort Chimo, QC.
GLENBOW MUSEUM NB-60-GM-2

INDIAN RESIDENTIAL SCHOOL, KUPER ISLAND, B.C.

Kuper Island Residential School, Kuper Island, BC. LAC 4674047

My sister died from TB (tuberculosis) when she was twelve and I was nine. Sadly, I hadn't been allowed to talk to her for the last five years since I had started Residential School."

The loss felt by families when children were taken to Residential School was multi-generational and took its toll on the wellness of not only families, but also the community.

Howard Stacy Jones was taken without his parents' knowledge from a public school in Port Renfrew, British Columbia, and sent to the Kuper Island Residential School.

"I was kidnapped from Port Renfrew's elementary school when I was around six years old, and this happened right in the elementary schoolyard. And my auntie witnessed this and another non-Native witnessed this, and they are still alive as I speak. These two witnesses

Family members camp outside the fence at Qu'Appelle Indian Industrial School in Lebret, SK, ca 1885. LAC PA182246

saw me fighting, trying to get away with, from the two RCMP officers that threw me in the back seat of the car and drove off with me. And my mom didn't know where I was for three days, frantically stressed out and worried about where I was, and she finally found out that I was in Kuper Island Residential School."

Family Visits

For the most part, family visits did not occur. When they did, there was limited privacy, and the visit had to be conducted in English so the nuns or priests and/or school staff could understand what was being said.

The above photo shows families camped outside the gate of the Qu'Appelle Indian Industrial School in Saskatchewan in 1885. Even though they were not allowed to talk to or touch

Reflections

What do you think happened to families, communities and the Nation when children were taken away to Residential School?

How would it impact parents and grandparents?

How would it impact the community as a whole?

their children, at least they could see them. This school was originally built to honour one of the conditions of Treaty 4. It burned to the ground in 1904, was rebuilt, burned again in 1932 and was rebuilt yet again. It operated until 1969.

Trips Home

While many students went home for the summers and sometimes at Christmas, some students stayed at the schools year-round. Frances Tait shares how the supervisor for the Alberni school would have a list of students who were going home for the summer.

"I remember hoping, crossing my fingers, crossing my toes that my name would be on that list, but it never was. And finally, one, one summer, I guess when I was about ten years old, I guess, in a way, I bet that I was thinking that maybe if I had a suitcase I would go home. So I went into the cloakroom, and I stole a suitcase and didn't put my name in it but put my brother's name in it and waited. And still, my name was not on that list. But because I stole the suitcase and because I had gone into the cloakroom without permission, I got punished. And it was to scrub the stairs from top to bottom with a toothbrush."

These students at All Saints Anglican Indian Residential School in Aklavik lived too far from the school to leave in the summer.
LAC 3193915

Fred's Journey

"I was taken to school when I was four. I was too young to go to classes, so I'd spend all day alone. When I was six years [old] I got tuberculosis in my left lung and had to go to the hospital. For years, I went back and forth between the hospital and the school, but to keep close check on my TB they kept me at school while the other students went home for summer and Christmas breaks. It was very lonely and scary to be left behind with those nuns.

"I received many beatings over those years and as a result, my right arm is permanently damaged and I only have about 50 percent functioning of it. Even though I don't remember much about those years, I do remember feeling scared most of the time. I also started to stutter. I stuttered for thirty-five years and was always very ashamed of my stuttering. Finally, I got healthier and stronger and my dream came true. I was allowed to return home during Christmas break. I was fifteen." ●

Photo: Monique Gray Smith

Leaving School

As you can imagine, leaving Residential School was a memorable day for most students. Yet for some, visiting home or finally getting out of Residential School for good had its own unique stresses. Students had often become disconnected from their families, their land and their culture and were often unable to communicate with their loved ones due to language barriers.

How do you think you would feel if you were taken from home at age four and never got to go back until you were fifteen?

What celebrations, events, holidays and family gatherings do you think you would miss out on?

A close-up of a traditional Métis sash.
FRED CATTROLL

Many students felt they not only didn't belong in their own communities, but that they didn't belong *anywhere*.

When Vitaline Elsie Jenner went home for the summer holidays from the Fort Chipewyan school in Alberta, she was ashamed of her ancestry. "In the summers, when I went home from the Residential School, I did not want to know my parents anymore. I was so programmed that at one time I looked down at my mom and dad, my family life, my culture, I looked down on it, ashamed, and that's how I felt." She tried to deny who she was. "I didn't want to be an Aboriginal person. No way did I want to be an Aboriginal person. I did everything. Dyed my hair and whatever else, you know, just so I wouldn't look like an Aboriginal person, denied my heritage, my culture, I denied it."

MÉTIS CHILDREN

Existing records make it impossible to say how many Métis children attended Residential School. Remember, it wasn't until 1982 and the rewriting of the constitution that the federal government officially acknowledged Métis as Indigenous people. This meant that policies for Residential School, both at federal and provincial/territorial levels, were unclear when it came to the enrolment of Métis children. There were few public schools in Métis communities,

Teacher Jennie Wright and her class of Métis students, 1950.
CANADIAN MUSEUM OF HISTORY, IMAGE 2002-2

and if parents wanted their children to have a formal education, often their only choice was to try to have their children attend a Residential School. Thanks to the work of the TRC and the Métis Survivors and their families, we now know that Métis children attended almost every Residential School and had the same experiences—limited diets, crowded and unsanitary housing, harsh discipline, heavy workloads, neglect and abuse.

INUIT CHILDREN

Some of the earliest forms of Residential Schools were tents and hostels that were set up across the North, although they were not officially seen as Residential Schools. For many

Inuit children were housed in tents at the Coppermine Tent Hostel. THE GENERAL SYNOD ARCHIVES, ANGLICAN CHURCH OF CANADA

> **"We haven't talked about the sacredness of the choice of parenting that was made in the spirit world. That was a sacred covenant. That sacred bond was broken when children were taken away for school. It can never be repaired, and so how wounded is that mom and father, and what do those wounds look like in daily life."**
> **Diane Longboat**

years, the Inuit were able to avoid Residential Schools. This was because until 1939 they were not considered Indians by the federal government, so they weren't governed by the Indian Act. Once all this changed, the first government-run Residential School for Inuit children opened in 1951. By 1964, 75 percent of Inuit children were attending Residential Schools.

RIPPLE EFFECT

The effect of Residential Schools continues to be felt in homes, jails and institutions across this country. Poverty, child-welfare interactions, incarceration and school drop-out and suicide rates are disproportionately higher among Indigenous people than they are in the rest of Canadian society.

This quote from "The Essence of Formation," by Ernest Larson, gives us insight into how sometimes an individual who has been abused can become an abuser, and how abuse impacts Indigenous communities across the country.

> *What we live, we learn.*
> *What we learn, we practice.*
> *What we practice, we become.*
> *And, what we become has consequences.*

A Mrs. Haggerty takes three Inuit children to school in Yellowknife, NWT, ca 1970.
LAC PA136743

Elder Kahontakwas (Diane Longboat) of the Turtle Clan in the Kanienkehaka Nation reminds us of the sacredness of the relationship between parent and child. "We haven't talked about the sacredness of the choice of parenting that was made in the spirit world. That was a sacred covenant. That sacred bond was broken when children were taken away for school. It can never be repaired, and so how wounded is that mom and father, and what do those wounds look like in daily life."

As you can imagine, a large number of Indigenous people in Canada are **intergenerational Survivors**, and the effect on them is complex.

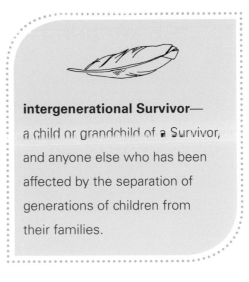

intergenerational Survivor— a child or grandchild of a Survivor, and anyone else who has been affected by the separation of generations of children from their families.

> "We are the first generation that didn't go to Residential School, but we sure lived it at home. We are still living it at home, and we are often forgotten about. Of course the Survivors need support and healing, but how do the future generations come together to heal, heal our dysfunctional ways? We lived it at home, and are still living it."
> **Chastity Davis**

Generations of Indigenous women celebrate honesty, love, kindness and reciprocity. MONIQUE GRAY SMITH

Parenting

One of the greatest impacts of Residential Schools became evident when Survivors began to have their own children. Growing up as they had, separated from their own parents and extended families, the majority of students knew very little about how to parent, show affection, care for and love a child. One student, who attended school in northern Ontario in the 1960s, was fifteen when she got married. "I didn't know anything. I was sixteen when I had my first child. No one ever told me what to expect. I didn't feel connected to my parents or anybody. I wasn't told anything, I wasn't told anything about how to raise, raise my children."

In the schools there were "unwritten rules" that the students learned to follow. They were:

Don't talk.

Don't trust.

Don't feel.

Don't love.

Mi`kmaq mother with seven children in Whycocomagh, NS.
COURTESY OF THE NOVA SCOTIA MUSEUM

Victoria McIntosh, who was at the Fort Alexander school in Manitoba, says, "If you didn't have older siblings to protect you, you're on your own, so you learned how to, to fight, anger, and not trusting anybody, and just being hard, you know, and you weren't gonna cry, and if you cried then that was not a good thing, and it was a sign of being weak. But I always felt, like, inside that I hated, I hated all of that. I never wanted to intentionally hurt anybody."

The "rules" permeated families for generations, but today we are seeing people learning new ways…ways that support them openly expressing their feelings instead of numbing them. Trust is being built, and individuals and families are learning to share and express their love.

Addictions

Addictions to alcohol, drugs, sex, gambling and food, to name just a few, swept through communities for generations. In many ways it is easy to understand why. Remember the belief that raising children is a sacred responsibility? Well, what happens to the parents, grandparents, aunts and uncles of a community when all the children are taken to Residential School? Where is their purpose? To whom do they pass on the stories, teachings and legends? How do they deal with the incredible grief? Do you think it is possible that this kind of grief caused people to attempt to numb the pain with alcohol and drugs? And what about the children who experienced abuse at the school? When they got out, how did they cope with the nightmares and memories that haunted them—especially since Residential Schools weren't talked about much in our families, communities and in our country until the mid-1990s? Do you think it is possible the Survivors, too, would have turned to alcohol or other things to numb the pain and try to forget?

Keith's Journey

Keith Matthew is from the Simpcw First Nation in British Columbia. He is a former chief, an intergenerational Residential School Survivor, a father and a businessman. He loves to spend time on the land and is an athlete who plays fastball and hockey.

"Reconciliation to me is the history of my family and, more importantly, the history of my mom and my dad. My dad Wilf Matthew, and my mom Delores Matthew (Jules), they went to Kamloops Indian Residential School. As far as I know they both went to grade eight. It was such a devastating time for our people. It left an indelible mark on me as an intergenerational person who was caught up in a lot of the unresolved issues of Residential School.

"My dad was born in 1919 and my mom was born ten years later. My dad was particularly hurt by his experience in Residential School and his favourite saying was 'I'm the most even-tempered man in the world. I'm mad all the time.' And it really did describe my dad.

"Regardless of the way he was, I loved him and I loved my mother.

"Quite honestly, because of the Residential School both of my parents were alcoholics, and all of the negative things that went along with alcoholism were endemic in my home. All those negative things that happened in my house; it scarred me emotionally, physically, mentally, spiritually. Not so much the physically, but the other three areas especially. I was

Photo compliments of Gail Joe/Focusin

depressed a lot when I was growing up. That can be normal as a teenager, but you add the stress of living in a dysfunctional household and it multiples tenfold.

"I think there are some really good things that we can do about reconciling our pasts and trying to work together as Canadians. I always see myself as hyphenated Canadian; I see myself as a Secwepmec-Canadian because my people are the ones I count on when the chips are down and when things are bad.

"Reconciliation is a fairly complex notion because the history of Canada is complex. Indigenous and Canadian relations are very complex and so it requires a complex answer. ●

Now that you know a bit about Residential Schools, please take a few minutes to complete the following sentences:

I knew…
Now I know…
I used to think…
Now I think…
I used to feel…
Now I feel…

moral courage—the courage to take action, even if there will be consequences, because you feel it is the right thing to do.

SPEAKING OUT

As you've read this book, perhaps you have found yourself wondering, Why didn't anyone do anything? Someone had to have known what was going on. Why didn't anyone speak up or try to stop this?

> **"Dr. Bryce stood up for the safety, health and well-being of First Nations, Métis and Inuit children...We want others to follow his example by having the courage to stand up for the right thing and help this generation of First Nations, Métis and Inuit children and youth have the same chance to succeed as other children and youth in Canada."**
> **First Nations Child & Family Caring Society of Canada**

Yes, there were people who attempted to raise awareness about Residential Schools and create change. There were people who had the **moral courage** to speak out. One of them was Dr. Peter Bryce, a pioneer in public health. In 1907 he toured schools in Western Canada and was shocked at the health of the students. He wrote a report on the state of the schools, citing an average death rate of 40 percent of children in the schools. He called the health conditions in the schools a "national crime."

On November 15, 1907, Dr. Bryce's report was quoted in the *Ottawa Citizen*. To view the story, please visit canadiangenocide.nativeweb.org/keynewsschoolsandwhiteplague.html.

His report was never released to the public, and in 1909 Dr. Bryce was removed from his job at the Department of Indian Affairs. In 1922 he published his report under the title *The Story of a National Crime: Being a Record of the Health Conditions of the Indians of Canada from 1904 to 1921.*

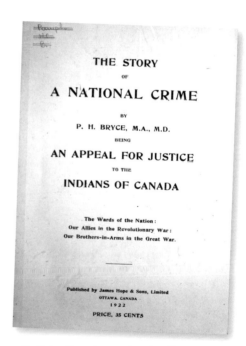

Dr. Peter Bryce's report on health conditions in Residential Schools was never released to the public. ARCHIVES.ORG

·3·

LOVE
Where Do We Stand Today?

> "The only way we are going to change the conditions we have created in the world is to create a wave of love energy that will sweep the face of the earth and be more beautiful than the evil trying to take over the world. You define what that love energy means to you."
>
> **Elder Kahontakwas (Diane Longboat),**
> Turtle Clan, Kanienkehaka Nation

Love is not a word that comes up often when Survivors describe how they felt and what they experienced at school. It makes sense, then, that one of the best ways to heal the wounds from those schools is to focus on love.

A key part of our country's journey of reconciliation is learning to love each other. I don't mean in a romantic way, but in a way that is rooted in respect and honours the uniqueness of each individual. This is critical because respect and honour were rarely part of the Residential School experience.

The importance of love kept coming up in interviews I read and in those I've had the privilege of conducting. I heard Elders and Traditional Knowledge Keepers refer to love as medicine. Think about that. If love is a form of medicine, then it is without question one of the medicines we need in this country to heal the wounds of Residential Schools.

Now that you've read about the history of Residential Schools, you may feel ashamed that they existed in our country. We must learn from the atrocities that occurred and ensure that children and families are never treated in such harmful ways again. This is why reconciliation is critical at this time in our country, and why young people are fundamental partners in our journey forward.

In this chapter, I will share with you the journey of the Truth and Reconciliation Commission of Canada (TRC), which spanned six years and produced 94 Calls to Action. You will read interviews with both young people and Elders from across Canada, who answered questions about history, what reconciliation means to them and what they hope for our country. Their responses and definitions of reconciliation are as unique as the individuals themselves.

Photo: Shari Nakagawa

The courage of Survivors and their families in sharing their stories of Residential Schools, the work of the Truth and Reconciliation Commission and the visionary work of many allies across our country have provided the foundation of reconciliation that we are now working from.

WHAT DOES RECONCILIATION MEAN?

Before we learn more about the Truth and Reconciliation Commission, let's look at what reconciliation means to some of the people I interviewed for this book.

Young Voices

It means fixing something, something that is broken or something that went wrong. It's like apologizing, but in a much bigger manner. So far, reconciliation has been okay in our country, but I think we can do more. It's never enough. We can keep improving and taking a step further.
—**Sahej, 11**

Sadie A-M and Frances. SHARI NAKAGAWA

It means to recognize what has happened, but we haven't really recognized it.
—**Jade, 13**

It means that people are going to get their stories out and there will be healing and people will get better.
—**Amelia, 11**

Sahej and Isabelle. SHARI NAKAGAWA

First I took a big guess at it, and this is what spilled out of my heart: mending bonds, fences and relationships. Finding ways to cooperate and create harmony. Extend an apology for hurting someone and then moving forward to creating a healthy relationship.
—**Natasha, 12**

The process of reconciliation in which a person has committed a wrong apologizes, tries to make up for the wrongs. It's interesting the reconciliation process has definitely started, but it needs more momentum.
—**Liam, 13**

To me it means like moving forward. We need to move forward as a country. If there is something in the past you did wrong, something big like Residential Schools, we need to deal with [it].
—**Maddy, 11**

It's hard to define, but to me it means remembering and not denying past events.
—**Mirabella, 12**

Maddy and Amelia. SHARI NAKAGAWA

Looking at all that has happened and looking into what will happen in the future.
—**Gabe, 13**

Get together and know more about each other and come together.
—**Amber, 9**

Older Voices

We are all one. We are all connected. The good parts in me are the good parts in you and the bad parts in you are the bad parts in me. We have things to learn from each other, and when we can do that, we can make huge changes.
—**Chastity Davis, entrepreneur**

It means acknowledging the role and responsibility that the Anglo community has historically in the injustices that took place. Reconciliation is acknowledging we have to respect that things need to be done differently and that there is a price to that, and it's a price we should be willing to pay."
—**Craig Knight, grandfather, retired public servant**

Reconciliation means helping our communities heal from the negative impacts of Residential Schools, colonialism and all of the things that have hurt us as Aboriginal people. Reconciliation means acknowledging the negative history. We (First Nations) have a responsibility too: not to be victims.
—**Keith Matthew, businessperson**

For me, reconciliation would be normalization of respectful relationships between Indigenous and non-Indigenous peoples of Canada.
—**Dr. Marie Wilson, TRC commissioner**

Reconciliation is asking myself who my Ancestors were the day before they went to Residential School, then doing everything I can to return to that.
—**Ryan McMahon, creator of the *Red Man Laughing* podcast**

At the very basis it's an agreement of a shared hope to move forward, but that can't happen unless there's an agreement and understanding of the past and what has actually happened in the past. That is the heart of reconciliation. —**Jennifer Manuel, author, founder of TRC Reading Challenge**

Reconciliation can be emotional, spiritual, cognitive, but for me it boils down to a power issue. It is about positioning our people in our own homeland in an equitable place of power and decision-making.
—**Elder Kahontakwas (Diane Longboat), Turtle Clan, Kanienkehaka Nation**

Reconciliation means action, not words, and trust building. Reconciliation is a learning and healing journey, and on this journey we—those who are visitors here—take our guidance from you, those whose lands we are visitors upon."
—**Lisa Helps, mayor of Victoria, BC**

THE INDIAN RESIDENTIAL SCHOOLS SETTLEMENT AGREEMENT

In the 1980s, Survivors began coming forward with stories about what had happened to them in Residential Schools. They wanted the federal government and the churches to take responsibility for the abuse they had experienced while at school, so they started legal actions. These cases went all the way to the Supreme Court of Canada. In the Blackwater case, the Supreme Court ruled that "if a child has been injured in the school by somebody working in the school, then the government and the church running that school can be sued for the injury to the child."

This ruling created an opportunity for Survivors to seek justice. In 2005, Phil Fontaine, National Chief of the Assembly of First Nations, announced a class-action lawsuit against the Government of Canada over the legacy of the Residential Schools. Eventually an out-of-court settlement was reached. It is known as the Indian Residential Schools Settlement Agreement (IRSSA)—the largest class action settlement in Canadian history. The IRSSA is an attempt by the federal government, the churches, and the Survivors to address the legacy of the Indian Residential School system. Five billion dollars was allocated as a compensation fund. The agreement included First Nations, Inuit and Métis Residential School students.

Phil Fontaine, the former national chief of the Assembly of First Nations. Photo by David Martin.

In May 2006, all parties—the Government of Canada, the Assembly of First Nations, and the Catholic, Anglican and United Churches—approved the agreement. The IRSSA identified five elements to address the legacy of Indian Residential Schools.

1. A Common Experience Payment (CEP) for all eligible former students of Indian Residential Schools. Eighty thousand former students made claims to this fund for compensation for being removed from their families, their communities, their culture, their language and their land.

2. An Independent Assessment Process (IAP) for claims of sexual or serious physical abuse. Thirty-seven thousand former students came forward with claims.

3. Measures to support healing, such as the Indian Residential Schools Resolution Health Support Program and an endowment to the Aboriginal Healing Foundation.

4. Commemorative activities.

5. The establishment of a truth and reconciliation commission.

The 17-meter (55-foot) Reconciliation Pole was installed at the University of British Columbia in Vancouver, BC, on April 1, 2017. The pole was carved by Haida master carver and hereditary Chief James Hart (7idansuu). Photo by Paul Joseph/UBC Communications & Marketing.

Almost half of the surviving students who went to Residential School testified that they were harmed in some way while they were at school and that the harm had long-term consequences. The families of students who had already died could not access the settlement money. There was no justice for the dead, their families and the communities attempting to heal the trauma of their members.

APOLOGY

History was made in Canada on June 11, 2008, when then-prime minister Stephen Harper made a public apology for the government's role in Indian Residential Schools. "I stand before you today to offer an apology to former students of Indian Residential Schools. The treatment of children in Indian Residential Schools is a sad chapter in our history...On behalf of the government of Canada and all Canadians, I stand before you, in this chamber so central to our life as a country, to apologize to aboriginal peoples for Canada's role in the Indian Residential Schools system...We now recognize that it was wrong to separate children from rich and vibrant cultures and traditions, that it created a void in many lives and communities, and we apologize for having done this. We now recognize that, in separating children from their families, we undermined the ability of many to adequately parent their own children and sowed

I stand before you today to offer an apology to former students of Indian Residential Schools. The treatment of children in Indian Residential Schools is a sad chapter in our history...We now recognize that it was wrong to separate children from rich and vibrant cultures and traditions.
Prime Minister Stephen Harper, June 11, 2008

Reflections

What does it mean to apologize?

Is an apology the words said or the actions taken or both?

the seeds for generations to follow and we apologize for having done this...The burden of this experience has been on your shoulders for far too long. The burden is properly ours as a government, and as a country."

This apology was met with varied reactions, depending on personal and family experience with Residential Schools and their continued influence on children, families and communities.

Some people felt that the prime minister's words were not sincere, and they experienced very little positive affirmation as a result of the apology. Others, like Fred John, felt the apology had a profound impact. "When I heard the Prime Minister apologize, something happened in my brain and I can speak my language again. I know it sounds crazy, but it's true."

THE TRUTH AND RECONCILIATION COMMISSION

As part of the IRSSA, the Truth and Reconciliation Commission of Canada (TRC) was launched in 2009. When the commission, Elders, advisors and staff, along with representatives from the Survivors and the members of the parties to the settlement agreement, gathered for the first time, one of their initial tasks was to come up with a working definition of reconciliation. As they brainstormed and shared their personal definitions of reconciliation, they came up with 128

Truth and Reconciliation
Commission of Canada

Indigenous leaders gather to hear Prime Minister Stephen Harper's apology in the House of Commons in June 2008. Granny Wabano (left, with cane) was the oldest living Residential School Survivor. She died in 2015 at the age of 111. REUTERS / ALAMY STOCK PHOTO

different definitions. Wow! That gives you a sense of how complex reconciliation can be.

In the end, the TRC defined reconciliation as "an ongoing process of establishing and maintaining respectful relationships" between Indigenous and non-Indigenous people that "will require commitment from all those affected including First Nations, Inuit and Métis former Indian Residential School (IRS) students, their families, communities, religious entities, former school employees, government and the people of Canada."

At the TRC Alberta National Event in Edmonton, March, 2014. Left to right, Commissioner Marie Wilson, Justice Murray Sinclair, Don Iveson (Mayor of Edmonton and TRC Honorary Witness), Commissioner Wilton Littlechild.

The goals of the commission were clearly laid out, and three commissioners were appointed— chairperson Justice Murray Sinclair and commissioners Chief Wilton Littlechild and Dr. Marie Wilson, all highly respected and known for their integrity and compassion.

The work the commissioners did for six years was emotional, intense, exhausting and demanding, not only of them, but also of their families. To support them and their wellness, each commissioner chose a spiritual advisor to walk with them through the course of their work.

As well, a ten-member Indian Residential Schools Survivor Committee, made up of Residential School Survivors from across Canada, served as an advisory body to the TRC.

The TRC was responsible for:

‣ Providing a holistic, culturally appropriate and safe setting for former students, their families and communities in which to share their experiences with the Commission

‣ Preparing a complete historical record on the policies and operations of Residential Schools

> **"My role as a commissioner is a once-in-a-lifetime opportunity to contribute to building a better Canada, one that is inclusive of everyone."**
> **Chief Wilton Littlechild**, TRC commissioner, in *Cultural Survival Quarterly Magazine*, March 2011

- Completing a public report, including recommendations to the parties of the IRSSA

- Establishing a national research centre that would be a lasting resource about the Residential School legacy

- Hosting seven national events in different regions across Canada

- Supporting community events designed by individual communities to meet their unique needs

- Coordinating document collection and undertaking specific research to be incorporated into the TRC Report and the National Research Centre

- Supporting public education through outreach, media and communication efforts

Flotillas of cedar dugout canoes marked the first major Reconciliation Week event in Vancouver, BC in September, 2013. NATIONAL CENTRE FOR TRUTH AND RECONCILIATION ARCHIVES, PHOTOGRAPH (BC NATIONAL EVENT): PHBCNE_00146, TRUTH AND RECONCILIATION COMMISSION OF CANADA

Statement Gathering

Anyone affected by the Residential School experience could share their story by providing a written or recorded statement, in a private, one-on-one interview or through a public discussion. Participation was voluntary, and participants could choose how they wanted to share.

‣ Commemorating Residential School Survivors and paying tribute in a lasting manner, in partnership with Indigenous and Northern Affairs Canada (INAC)

THE NATIONAL TRC EVENTS

The TRC was mandated "to receive statements and documents from former students, their families, community and all other interested participants," and to recognize "the unique experiences" of all former students. To that end, it hosted events all across the country to listen to Canadians who wanted to share their Residential School stories. The first TRC national event was held in Winnipeg, Manitoba, in 2010. The final national event took place in 2014 in Edmonton, Alberta, and the TRC's closing ceremonies were held in Ottawa, Ontario, in June 2015. In December 2015 the TRC released its report.

The national events engaged the Canadian public and provided education about the Residential School system, the experience of former students and their families, and the ongoing legacies of the schools. The events were held in seven large cities across the country, and the Seven Sacred Teachings guided these events. Each of the seven flames in the circle of the TRC's logo represents one of the Seven Sacred Teachings.

Regional events were also held across the country.

Event 1: Winnipeg, Manitoba—**RESPECT**

Event 2: Inuvik, Northwest Territories—**COURAGE**

Event 3: Halifax, Nova Scotia—**LOVE**

Event 4: Saskatoon, Saskatchewan—**TRUTH**

Event 5: Montréal, Québec—**HUMILITY**

Event 6: Vancouver, British Columbia—**HONESTY**

Event 7: Edmonton, Alberta—**WISDOM**

After becoming an Honourary Witness, Her Excellency Sharon Johnston (far left) took part in a talking circle moderated by Ms. Shelagh Rogers (with microphone) in June, 2015. SGT RONALD DUCHESNE, RIDEAU HALL, OSGG.© HER MAJESTY THE QUEEN IN RIGHT OF CANADA REPRESENTED BY THE OFFICE OF THE SECRETARY TO THE GOVERNOR GENERAL, 2015. REPRODUCED WITH THE PERMISSION OF THE OSGG, 2017.

HONOURARY WITNESSES

Witnessing is a term used in some Indigenous communities. Those who are called to witness are in many ways the keepers of history when an event of historic significance occurs. This is an important custom for many families and communities and is not only part of oral traditions. Witnessing requires us to be present and use our ears, our eyes and our hearts to witness and remember what has unfolded. Witnesses are requested to not only be keepers of the memory of their experience and the event, but also to share what they saw, felt, heard and experienced.

In many ways, what you are doing by reading this book is being a witness—a witness to the history, to the stories and the journeys.

Honourary Witnesses played a critical role in the TRC and will continue to play a critical role in our country as our journey of reconciliation continues.

honourary witness—someone who witnesses and remembers an event of historic significance and also shares what he or she saw, felt, heard and experienced.

Shelagh's Journey

Shelagh Rogers was one of the first Canadians invited to be an Honourary Witness. She is a journalist and the host of the CBC Radio show *The Next Chapter*. She is also the Chancellor of the University of Victoria.

Photo: UVic Photo Services

Shelagh still remembers the day the letter arrived from Dr. Marie Wilson, inviting her to be a witness to the testimony of what really happened in Canada to so many children.

For Shelagh, being an Honourary Witness meant "creating a circle of people that would witness the truth and always stand for the truth, so that no matter what, if you heard falsities being uttered you would stand up and say, 'That is not what happened. This is what happened.'" As an Honourary Witness, Shelagh takes on what she calls a sacred assignment.

Shelagh says, "There are many perspectives, but there is one story. That something bad happened here for very bad purposes, and for a very long period of time. I love my country, but I do not love its history, and I do not accept the myths that I grew up with."

Shelagh has been changed through her journey as an Honourary Witness. It has changed the way she participates in and sees the world. "I hear things differently. I read the paper differently. I make it a daily practice to do something that makes things a little bit better." ●

Indigenous young people sang, drummed and danced in the Walk for Reconciliation in Vancouver, BC, September, 2013. Photo by Yolanda Cole/Georgia Straight

Reflections

Where do you see yourself and your friends taking action?

Where do you see your school taking action?

Where do you see your community taking action?

94 CALLS TO ACTION

The "how to" part of reconciliation flowed from the commissioners' listening to 6,750 individuals who gave statements at national and regional gatherings, which resulted in 94 Calls to Action. These are outlined in the TRC's summary of the final report, released in June 2015. The TRC's mandate had originally said it would create *recommendations*, but the commissioners intentionally decided to call them calls to action. This change in wording is important—the TRC thought the word *recommendations* sounded optional, and they did not want the steps forward to be seen as optional.

I encourage you to either read the 94 Calls to Action on the TRC's website or go to YouTube (#94daysforreconciliation) and watch young people share the Calls to Action and how they understand them in their lives. The links are all on the website www.speakingourtruth.ca.

WALK FOR RECONCILIATION

On September 22, 2013, over 70,000 people braved the heavy rain in Vancouver, British Columbia, for the 4 km Walk for Reconciliation. The first reconciliation walk in Canada, it was seen as a walk for peace and a new way forward. Each step expressed a desire to rebuild and foster healthy relationships between Indigenous and non-Indigenous people. The Walk for Reconciliation was named the number two Top News Maker of the Year by CBC News Vancouver.

BARRIERS TO JUSTICE

In its investigations, the TRC found that Indian Affairs officials actively covered up the abuse of children at Residential Schools, allowed known abusers to remain near vulnerable children and interfered with police investigations.

Unfortunately, this subtle and pervasive keeping of secrets is not just in the distant past. Sometimes embarrassment and guilt push people to try to keep hiding problems and mistakes. Even after the schools were closed, official apologies were begun and efforts began to acknowledge the nation's history, attempts were made to hide information and control the story told about Canada.

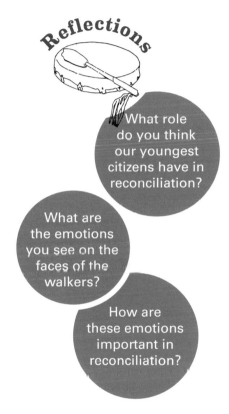

Reflections

What role do you think our youngest citizens have in reconciliation?

What are the emotions you see on the faces of the walkers?

How are these emotions important in reconciliation?

> **"Aboriginal children need to know about the history of their families, and non-Aboriginal Canadians need to know about the history of our country. What the Truth and Reconciliation Commission made clear is that the process is only just begun in Canada."**
>
> **Rupert Ross**, retired Ontario Crown attorney, author of *Indigenous Healing: Exploring Traditional Paths*

In 2011 the TRC found that the federal government was putting up "administrative barriers" that prevented the TRC from accessing historical documents. The barriers became so problematic that in late 2012 the Commission had to take the federal government to court for refusing to release millions of documents.

The Commission eventually gained access to the documents, but not without undue difficulty and challenge. It will take a completely different approach to heal the wounds that have been inflicted and remove barriers to true justice.

IN THE END…
OR PERHAPS THE BEGINNING

In all, 6,750 people gave recorded statements to the TRC. Most were given in private settings. Others were given at the national, regional and community events, at sharing circles or at hearings organized by the Commission. These private and public statements form a key part of the Commission's legacy.

While the TRC heard mostly from Survivors, the children and grandchildren of the Survivors came forward to make statements as well. As part of the "town halls" at TRC gatherings, non-Indigenous people were given opportunities to speak.

I encourage you to visit the National Centre for Truth and Reconciliation (NCTR) website (umanitoba.ca/nctr). You will find powerful videos there that will help you continue your journey of reconciliation.

While on the NCTR website, please also take time to look at the reports released in 2015 by the Truth and Reconciliation Commission.

LOVE

Let's bring this chapter to a close by coming full circle. At the beginning we talked about the importance of love and the traditional teaching of love in regards to reconciliation. Love is powerful, and love is medicine. I hope you remember that!

I'd like to invite you to end this section of your journey with a bit of homework. It's easy—trust me. It's an invitation to reconciliation and love…

One of the projects profiled in the next chapter is the *Red Man Laughing* podcast. In the Season 5 episode "The Murray Sinclair Keynote," Ryan McMahon shares words and stories from TRC chair Murray Sinclair. Go to 49:38 and you will hear a beautiful story of love. A true example of how love triumphs.

I hope you take time to listen. It is a beautiful way to end this section and prepare for what's next. Go to www.redmanlaughing.com and click on Season 5, then "The Murray Sinclair Keynote."

›4‹

KINDNESS AND RECIPROCITY

Where Do We Go from Here?

{ **"I hope that we can get past the time of Residential Schools and that we recognize how wrong it was and find ways to make it right."**
Jade }

Kindness affects everyone. When we are on the receiving end of an act of kindness, we may feel grateful or loved or inspired. And when we perform an act of kindness, well, some say it actually feels better than being on the receiving end. If you've been lucky enough to witness an act of kindness, which I hope you have, you also know that witnessing such an act feels good. This is why in many cultures kindness is highly regarded.

When we look at Canada's history, we see a lack of kindness.

◄ Photo: iStock.com

Yellowknife Cultural Crossroads (1999) is an on-site sculpture project conceived and coordinated by the Fédération Franco-Ténoise as a testament to close collaboration among Métis, Dene, Inuvialuit, English-Canadian, French-Canadian and Québec cultures and dedicated to all peoples of the North.
PHOTOSCANADA.COM

Reflections

What do you think would happen in our country if there was an increase of kindness between Indigenous and non-Indigenous people?

Reciprocity is often defined as "the mutual exchange of privilege," which can mean different things in different situations. In the context of this book, it is about how we behave in relationship with each other. In reciprocal relationships, everyone benefits and has the same privileges, and people repay what another has provided to them. Reciprocity is like an unwritten rule—we need to treat people the way we want to be treated. Some of you may know this as the Golden Rule.

I included reciprocity as one of the traditional teachings in this last chapter because when we look at the history of Residential Schools, and specifically the courage and generosity of the

> **"By establishing a new and respectful relationship between Aboriginal and non-Aboriginal Canadians, we will restore what must be restored, repair what must be repaired, and return what must be returned."**
>
> *What We Have Learned: Principles of Truth and Reconciliation*, TRC

Survivors in sharing their stories, it calls on all of us to move forward with the same courage and generosity of spirit.

Near the end of its work, the TRC released a report called *What We Have Learned: Principles of Truth and Reconciliation*. In it there is a blueprint for reciprocity. This is how we need to live now.

A Message from Dr. Marie Wilson

Dr. Wilson and I met in Edmonton, and I had the privilege of visiting with her for over three hours. During that time I asked her numerous questions about her role as a TRC commissioner, mother, grandmother, wife of a Residential School Survivor, and citizen of Canada. At the end of our visit I had over eight pages of notes, and I then had the difficult task of choosing what to share with you. Here is some of what she said.

Dr. Marie Wilson. TRC

"I want to say something to young people, and that is that an awful lot of times we frame our society as if young people are the learners and adults have all the answers. I think what the work of the Truth and Reconciliation Commission and the story of Residential Schools tell us is two really

> **"I think children and young people can lead the way by telling Canada what they expect of us."**
>
> **Dr. Marie Wilson**

Reflections

Have you spoken up or taken action about something important to you?

How did it feel?

Can you describe a time when it was difficult for you to be honest?

How did it feel?

What do you think is the difference between honesty and being truthful?

important things. One is that adults can make terrible mistakes. Adults can get things very, very wrong. These schools existed because people who had a lot of power and a lot of influence thought it was okay to do this, to remove children from their homes. I haven't met anyone today that agrees that that was a good thing to have done.

"The other thing is, young people have tremendous things to contribute. They're really smart, they're really kind, and they can speak plainly and see plainly the things that adults sometimes skirt around. I think children and young people can lead the way by telling Canada what they expect of us. By telling elected leaders what they expect of them, by telling teachers what they expect to be taught, by telling their parents how they expect them to talk about other people. So I think children and young people have a tremendous amount to contribute." ●

BUILDING BRIDGES

Now that you have heard the stories of the Residential School Survivors, you understand the impact the schools had on generations of Indigenous people. You know why we are on this reconciliation journey. I hope you see that we have a beautiful opportunity for profound

change. But it isn't going to be easy, and it isn't up to the government to make the changes. It is up to each and every one of us!

Our work is to build the bridges. Each of us has a role in the bridge building in this country.

You know that reconciliation means different things to different people, families, communities and organizations. This is a good time to check in and remind yourself what reconciliation means to you—at least, what it means to you right now, because what reconciliation means to you today might be different next week or a year from now. That is the beauty of reconciliation. It is an ongoing journey.

Ideally, it means we continue growing, healing, learning and finding our way forward as a country. Reconciliation is critical in building an

> "**Reconciliation is really about relationships, and it boils down to this: I want to be your friend, and I want you to be mine. I want you to have my back. I want you to help me when I need help, and I want you to be able to call upon me when you need mine.**"
> **Justice Murray Sinclair**, TRC chair, accepting 2015 Duff Roblin Award, November 2015

inclusive and just society. It is a way forward that both honours our history *and* holds up the gifts of the Indigenous people and the non-Indigenous people of this country. It means building meaningful relationships with Indigenous and non-Indigenous people.

A Message from Elder Kahontakwas (Diane Longboat)

Over the years, I have had the privilege of working with and being in ceremony led by Diane. I have learned a great deal from her and am grateful for and inspired by all she shares with me.

When I think of allies, I think of our original relationships with one another as Indigenous Nations on Turtle Island. We maintained peaceful relations among Nations, resolved conflict through Councils, lacrosse and other medicine games, shared resources, valued giving over receiving and upheld each other as Nations with respect, friendship and honour. That's how it was among our people before the tenants arrived at the time of colonization.

Elder Kahontakwas (Diane Longboat)
MICHAEL O'BRIEN PHOTOGRAPHY

"Youth need to fall in love with creation as much as Indigenous Nations have."

Elder Kahontakwas (Diane Longboat)

Reconciliation means coming into right relationship with one another. This includes our relationship with the land.

The early wampum belts and agreements made between Indigenous Nations prior to contact talked about each Nation's territory as well as shared territory. In Ohio and part of Pennsylvania, shared territory meant all Nations benefitted from the rich hunting, fishing, wild food sources and medicines. The land was seen as a dish with one spoon that could feed all Nations. Not one particular Nation could lay claim to this land, or live there, but all surrounding Nations were richly fed from its abundance.

We all acknowledged the wealth of the abundance on the land, and we approached it with gratitude, using ceremonial offerings and giving thanks to the Creator in many languages of the Nations. Natural laws specify that one never takes the first thing one is seeking—the first deer, the first medicine. The law says one only takes what is needed and uses it all, without wasting anything.

Youth today need land-based learning so they can fall in love with creation as much as Indigenous Nations have. They have to see Mother Earth as

DESIGN PICS INC./ALAMY STOCK PHOTO

feeding them and providing them with a love energy that is nourishment for life. If youth are going to be allies for First Nations, youth have to see themselves as being part of creation. They are no better than or lesser than, and they have a specific duty to fulfill with the gifts that the Creator has given to each human being. If youth do not fall in love with creation, they will never defend the land or the beings of creation.

Inuit girls work together to build an igloo.
FRED CATTROLL

City life creates a nature-deficit disorder. It is important for their mental and emotional health that young people get out on the land. When we are on the land, the hierarchical structures become nonsensical, non-functional, meaning everyone and everything is equal. To be on the land, to survive, to thrive on the land, means you have to be able to work together as family, clan and community. You will see that every single person has a right to life, that everyone is unique and that every single person has a contribution to make to sustaining life. There is an action-oriented piece that goes along with these words. Taking action is the necessary element for reconciliation. I encourage young people to become actively engaged with First Nations organizations and youth councils.

Jay Charlie, a young member of the Vuntut Gwitchin First Nation, holds his hunted ptarmigan near Old Crow, YT. DEDDEDA WHITE

Learn about our shared issues, enrich your hearts and minds by asking questions, be curious, be bold. Question history, see the point of view of who is telling the story, and question motive.

Believe in a power that is greater than yourself, that there is a loving, caring Creator, hearing every single prayer. The only way we are going to change the conditions we have created in the world is to create a wave of love energy that will sweep the face of the earth and be more beautiful than the evil trying to take over the world. You define what that love energy means to you.

Believe in a future where we celebrate our common humanity but also celebrate our differences as beauty. ●

Photo: Shari Nakagawa

TALKING RECONCILIATION

It is important to me that young readers hear from other young people who are beginning to understand history in a different way and as a result are asking, "What can I do?"

When I interviewed young people, one of the things that surprised me most was how little they had been taught at school about Residential Schools. As always, there were exceptions, and as you read you will see just how powerful it can be when teachers and schools are active in educating students about the history and fostering reconciliation.

The majority of the young people I talked to were learning about the schools at home, which is exciting! It means that conversations are happening around the dinner table or while listening to the radio (usually CBC) or simply while being together as family.

I interviewed young people from Victoria, Toronto, Vancouver, Whitehorse, Saskatoon and Edmonton. I am immensely grateful to these youth! On the days when writing this book was emotionally painful and I felt like I just couldn't do it anymore, I would go back to my interviews with the youth. Their answers, their thoughtfulness, their wisdom and their hope for our country fuelled me to keep writing.

When I wrote this section, I imagined kids from all over the country sitting around a campfire, having a conversation about reconciliation. Some of them you have already met as they shared their journeys with you. I'll introduce the rest of them to you the way they describe themselves.

Gabe is Coast Salish. His dad is from Tsartlip, and his mom is of kʷakʷaǩwakʷ ancestry. Gabe's great-grandfather, grandfather, grandmother and one of his uncles went to Residential School.

Amelia is Ojibwe, with Jewish and Singaporian ancestry. Her great-grandma went to Residential School.

Jade is Anishinabe Kwe.

Liam is of German and Irish ancestry.

Amber is Anishinabe Kwe.

Mirabella is of Italian ancestry.

What have you learned about Residential Schools at home?

Gabe: We don't talk about Residential Schools much—it usually comes up when we have school projects. Mostly I know what bad it has brought, like the kids were stolen from their homes and forced to speak a different language. If we start with my grandfather on my dad's side, I'd have to say it's quite a lot different from how my dad's been raising us. My grandfather really struggled with how to raise his children; he wanted to fight for them and has fought the government for equality for our people. My grandmother was raised on Alert Bay, where they had St. Michael's, and she went there. For most of the time she'd play hooky and not go. My parents try not to raise my sister and I the way their parents did, or at least not the not-so-good things. Neither of them smoke, they don't drink, and they are raising us differently. My grandparents only raised my parents the way they were raised in Residential School.

Amelia: I learned there was lots of abuse. My great-grandma was in Residential School for a couple years. The clothes that parents and grandmas packed for the children were thrown away, and they put the powder that kills bugs in their hair.

Jade: I've learned a lot at home. I've learned the children were taken from families and forced to live at school. The schools took away culture, language, and cut the children's hair. The children couldn't see their family. My grandparents went to Residential School and because of that it's had lots of impacts on my dad and our family.

Liam: A fair bit—we listen to the radio a lot. The Residential School program was proposed as an education program to educate the Native people in the Western ways—they thought it was better. The system itself failed, and a lot of abuse happened. I find it so interesting when you learn about what happened that people thought they were doing the best thing for the kids back then. People took advantage of the system and did pretty atrocious things.

Amber: I've learned that they would take the children away from their parents and how they would not be so nice and they would not be fair.

There was abuse, hurting the kids for speaking their language. If they cried, they'd hurt them again or put them in the closet. They wouldn't let you be who you are. You couldn't be proud of who you are!

Mirabella: I've mostly learned about Residential Schools through my mom. The children would be taken away from their homes at a very young age and forced to become like white people. They were expected to know how to speak English, how to act like a white person, and if they ever spoke their language or of their traditional ways they would be brutally punished, in horrible ways. Horrible. The children could only see their families or go home over the summer. The rest of the time was at school.

What have you learned about Residential Schools at school?
Gabe: We haven't learned much about it at school, mostly through family.

Amelia: I learned that if one girl looked whiter than others, she would be favoured. There would still be discrimination, but she would be favoured. They would eat powdered food, mush and cabbage soup, while the nuns were eating bacon and eggs that the youth had made. We studied the Truth and Reconciliation Commission, and the history and stories. I've found it interesting learning about all of what has happened to the Aboriginal people—the horrible truth. I wasn't shocked; I don't know why, but I wasn't.

Jade: We have learned almost nothing about Residential Schools. We've gone over it for maybe five minutes, that's all.

Liam: We never really did much social studies last year or studying Native people. So my learning has been at home, on the radio and with my parents.

Amber: Not really talking about it at school, not yet. I'd like to learn more about it.

Mirabella: It's not a large topic that's been brought up very many times. We did a field trip, but not as a general topic that we have focused on for a long period of time. I wish it was a topic we were educated on so it's not forgotten about. I wish we'd learn more about the history.

What do you hope for our country?

Gabe: I'm really hoping that we stop all the racism, be able to put the schools behind us and think about what we can do to stop it from happening again. We don't want history to repeat itself.

Amelia: I hope we can all work together with Aboriginal people. We can learn to be better, to not be racist and not make rude comments. I think I can help people understand that the things they thought about Aboriginal people are wrong. There is real culture, beliefs, beautiful stories and a beautiful love for nature. I want to help people understand this was their original country and we are just living on the land.

Jade: I hope that we can get past the time of Residential Schools and that we recognize how wrong it was and find ways to make it right.

Liam: I hope we can get along with each other, but given humans' track record it's going to take a few years. If you think about the one-out-of-ten thing—one person does something wrong and we think it doesn't matter or doesn't affect the other nine, but it does matter. It's the same with doing good. That one thing matters.

Amber: I hope that we can come together in a good way and learn more about Residential Schools and the right things about First Nations. That there was peace and that people wouldn't fight as much as they do now. This would give us a better country than now.

Mirabella: I really hope that soon the country won't be as racist and excluding as it was and is now. We need to learn to accept each other. We're different, but just barely. We're all humans, the same species. Yet we're a species that hasn't learned to accept itself as of today.

Sahej's Journey

Sahej is of Indo-Canadian ancestry, and his family invited me to their home to interview him. When I met with Sahej, he had just turned eleven. I quickly came to know that his home is full of love.

Sahej first learned about Residential Schools in grade four. He learned about how the children were treated at the schools and why the children were treated that way. Sahej was shocked.

"It seemed like a nightmare. It didn't seem Canadian—it didn't seem possible in a country like this. There is one thing called cultural genocide, which is kind of like suicide, but of your culture. It is the killing of culture." Sahej learned that the Residential Schools tried to take the Indigenous culture and language out of each child.

When Sahej started to learn about Residential Schools and came home to have conversations with his parents, he was surprised to learn that they knew very little about Residential Schools. "I thought they would've learned about it as a big thing that was happening in the moment. It was surprising to me that they didn't know."

When I asked him what reconciliation means to him, Sahej answered that it "means fixing something, something that is broken or something that went wrong. It's like apologizing, but in a much bigger manner." Sahej thinks that Canada has started the process of fixing, but that it is not over. In order for

Photo: Shari Nakagawa

> **"By standing up for what is right. It's like the ripple effect. If someone says something, then another person can branch off from that. The first idea is like a seed for a tree, the next idea grows the trunk, and then the branches and then the leaves and then the fruit. In Canada and in reconciliation we are at the branch—the fruit hasn't come yet. When the fruit comes, our country will be much nicer to live in."**
> **Sahej**

Canada to reconcile, people need to keep improving and moving forward and becoming allies.

To Sahej, in order to be an ally you "need to understand the other person's point of view and you need to understand what's happening to them, not just what you think." Sahej thinks it also means standing up for others and standing up against hateful speech.

Sahej believes that one ally can make a change. "One person can make a difference. You don't have to have a big crowd with you. You can be one person and create a crowd. By standing up for what is right. It's like the ripple effect. If someone says something, then another person can branch off from that. The first idea is like a seed for a tree, the next idea grows the trunk, and then the branches and then the leaves and then the fruit. In Canada and in reconciliation, we are at the branch—the fruit hasn't come yet. When the fruit comes, our country will be much nicer to live in." ●

Maddy's Journey

When I interviewed Maddy, who is of English, French and Irish ancestry, she was almost eleven. Our interview happened over the phone.

Maddy learned about Residential Schools when her class engaged in an inquiry project that lasted four months. She learned that children at Residential Schools were made to "scrub floors, clean bathrooms and most times wouldn't eat much, always cleaning and working," and if "parents didn't give their kids up, they could go to jail."

Maddy told me what she learned about how kids were treated at the schools. "As kids we need privacy, but there was not privacy for the kids at Residential Schools. The teachers were not nice to the kids, punishing them with whips or making them go naked in front of class." Maddy said she thinks that kind of treatment is torture, and that the kids who attended Residential Schools were not getting the care and attention they needed and deserved. "Lots of kids died during this time. Kids my age died. Kids ran away knowing that they might never make it home, but the potential of death was better than staying at the school. That is hard for me to imagine."

What happened at Residential Schools is hard for many to imagine. "The kids never got to have the wonderful memories with their families like I have. I've gotten to go to many places with my family, and the children of Residential School never had that. It was taken away from them." This is a difficult part of history for many to accept and understand, especially when you are proud of your country. "It was crazy to learn that one of the safest countries to live in did this to humanity. I never want to see this again in the future; it's a sad thing."

Maddy thinks that in order to move forward in the process of reconciliation, we "need to move forward as a country. If there is something in the past you did wrong, something big like residential

Photo: Lifetouch

schools, we need to deal with it." To Maddy, dealing with it means learning about and sharing history, so that awareness of the truth increases. "We are learning this now so it doesn't happen again in the future." Maddy thinks that the more people learn about this, the more comfort we can be to one another, and "awareness creates healing." ●

> **"Being an ally means that you contribute to the healing, not the hurting."**
> **Craig Knight**, grandfather, retired public servant

Sahej and Sadie Piper. SHARI NAKAGAWA

BEING AN ALLY

An **ally** is someone who not only commits to social equality but also informs him or herself on the issues. Allies work to support diverse groups even if they don't identify as members.

Allies sometimes make the mistake of thinking they know the way things *should* go. We are in a new time. A time when we acknowledge and learn and respect different protocols, traditions, ceremonies, ways of being, knowing and doing. A time when not just listening to each other but really *hearing* each other is critical to how we move forward as individuals, families, communities and as a country.

It is in the similarities that we find our common humanity. When we start sharing and listening to each other, we find out how much we have in common. It is in our differences that we find our similarities.

> **"An ally is someone who does not act on his or her own concept of what 'should' be done, but someone who listens deeply. The idea of listening deeply to me is you are listening with the attitude that you might be changed by what you hear. That's it... that's being an ally."**
>
> **Jennifer Manuel**, author, founder of the TRC Reading Challenge

The Qualities of an Ally

Being an ally means starting with an open heart so you can hear what is being shared with you. Often when we hear stories of injustice, **genocide** and abuse, it ignites within us a desire to help and support positive change. Becoming an ally starts the moment you decide to become an ally, but the work of an ally lasts a lifetime. Being an ally always involves knowing yourself. This includes knowing your place in society, including understanding and confronting your own **privilege.**

The qualities of an ally include:

▸ Having a sense of responsibility and care

▸ Being willing to speak up when something isn't right

▸ Discovering and continuing to understand, strengthen and share the gifts you've been blessed with (your natural attributes)

ally—a person, group or nation that is linked with and works together with another person, group or nation for a shared purpose.

genocide—deliberate and intended action to destroy a group of people.

privilege—any unearned benefit, right, opportunity or advantage given to a person or a group because of their identity (class, race, age, gender, sex, etc.).

Students working with Project of Heart create tiles to express what they have learned about Residential Schools.

NATIONAL CENTRE FOR TRUTH AND RECONCILIATION ARCHIVES, PHOTOGRAPH (BC NATIONAL EVENT): PHBCNE_00483, TRUTH AND RECONCILIATION COMMISSION OF CANADA

▸ Being of service

▸ Being a good listener

▸ Knowing the role and responsibilities of an ally

▸ Knowing your own privilege

▸ Understanding why a certain issue (in this case, Residential Schools and Indigenous people in Canada) stirs something in you and makes you want to become an ally

WHAT CAN YOU DO?

Perhaps one of the largest questions facing our country is how do we navigate a new relationship and move forward?

Mirabella's quote leads me to ask, what can *we* do? What can *you* do? By now, this is not a new question to you. It is one I've been asking you to think about since the first few pages of this book.

> **"We can't fix what's been done, but there are things we can do now."**
> **Mirabella**

Natasha's Journey

Natasha was twelve when I interviewed her. On her mom's side she is Ojibwe and Irish, and her dad is Eastern European. Natasha is an intergenerational Residential School Survivor. "My great-grandma went to a school in northern Ontario. It broke her spirit, her hope and her love of herself and her passion for her culture. She came out broken and mean-spirited, and then she hurt my grandma. The abuse was passed on to my mother, but my mom has made a very clear vow not to hurt or harm me."

Residential Schools are a well-known topic in Natasha's household. "I've learned about the extreme abuse—mental, emotional, sexual abuse." The subject can come up unexpectedly at home and "the smallest comment can grow into a conversation." At school she "learned that Residential Schools were damaging to our people, destroyed families, and now we have unhealthy generations—and that makes me very sad."

Natasha's school participated in the making of the video *Finding Heart*. At the beginning of the year, her principal "asked the entire school at assembly how many knew about Residential School. Out of six hundred students, only three or four of us raised our hands. After creating the video, we went from three to four knowing about Residential School to all six hundred students raising hands." This change was moving for the students and also moving for other community members. "Five Elders were there

Photo: Shannon Beauchamp

as witnesses and said, 'Thank you for believing me.' They were crying."

Natasha hopes that every child will learn the truth about Canadian history. "I hope that the next generation grows out of this racist and ignorant phase and grows a healthy bond and place where everyone gets along and is respectful with each other." Asked what message she has for other young people, Natasha put compassion as a priority. "Be kind to yourself and others. Seek help if you are having trouble or feeling sad about something."

To find out more about the project that Natasha's school participated in, visit www.youtube.com/watch?v=V1NQ_tgR_oA ●

I am sure you have plenty of ideas and likely have already taken steps of reconciliation! However, if you are looking for more ideas, here are a few…

‣ As a starting place, learn whose territory you live and go to school on. When you go to a new place, learn whose land you are visiting.

‣ Learn how the First Peoples where you live prefer to be identified.

‣ Have a conversation with your family at the dinner table about what you are learning about history, reconciliation and the kind of Canada you want to live in.

- Share what you have learned. Continue talking with friends and family about Canada's history and reconciliation.

- Read Indigenous authors, being sure to balance female and male authors. Most school districts have an Aboriginal Education Department, which often includes a library of books written by Indigenous authors.

Orange Shirt Day drumming ceremony at Merritt Secondary School in Merritt, BC.
MICHAEL POTESTIO/*MERRITT HERALD*

- Wear an orange shirt on September 30 or whenever your school honours this day. If no one at school is talking about Orange Shirt Day (see page 129) by the second week in September, share information with your teacher and/or principal and ask them to help make it happen.

- Dedicate 94 days to watch the #94DaysForReconciliation videos on YouTube.

- Choose one of the calls to action and commit to taking steps that reflect it.

Students at Clinton Elementary School in Burnaby, BC, decorated their gym with orange paper shirts for Orange Shirt Day. Photo: Jodie Wilson.

▸ If you are not learning Canada's collective history in class, please ask why. You don't need to do this in front of the class. Ask your teacher privately, and share with him or her why you think it's important that history be shared in a way that is respectful of the Indigenous experience. Share this book with your teacher.

▸ Stand up and call out racism.

▸ Email your elected officials at all levels of government—municipal, provincial and federal—and ask them what they are doing to foster reconciliation and how they are implementing the 94 Calls to Action.

In March, 2013 a group of Cree youth walked 1600 kilometers to bring attention to aboriginal issues on Parliament Hill in Ottawa, ON.

You don't have to hold a public demonstration about reconciliation, but if that is what you are called to do, then go for it! These are only a few examples of possible answers to the question "What can I do?" and your answer(s) will depend on you. There is no right or wrong answer, but please, when you have finished this book, find a new way or ways to stay on the journey!

If you find yourself struggling with ways to answer the question, trust me—you are not alone. Millions of Canadians are asking themselves the same question.

One thing I know for sure is that there is always an answer. And it is never "Nothing." *There is always something we can do.*

MESSAGES TO INSPIRE YOU ON YOUR JOURNEY

Find a way to work across the differences. Then you might feel and see what you have in common.

Mayor Lisa Helps, Victoria, BC

What I would like young people to understand is the importance of courage. If we want things to be different in our society, if we want it to be fair and just and equitable for everyone, then we have to have the courage to make it so.

Craig Knight

I think the first thing is for children to know the extreme importance of loving themselves; that they are created, as part of creation, and that they are unique in the entire history of the universe. We don't always get what we want from the people we want to get it from but that doesn't mean that we should ever doubt for a second our own self-worth and the importance of taking care of ourselves and living in a good way.

Dr. Marie Wilson

RECONCILIATION PROJECTS AND INITIATIVES

The work of reconciliation is continuing in our country and perhaps will need to continue for generations yet to come, especially when you remember that the schools operated for over 150 years.

I am going to share with you examples of just a few of the projects and initiatives that are going on across our country. I was truly inspired as I researched this subject. There are many, many exciting reconciliation projects and events happening—a whole book could be written about the work that is being done, and there's not room for everything here. I had the incredibly difficult task of identifying a few key projects. I encourage you to research further the ones that interest you. Perhaps you and your friends will even organize your own project or invite one of the following projects to come to your school or community.

The National Centre for Truth and Reconciliation

The National Centre for Truth and Reconciliation (NCTR) opened in the summer of 2015. It was created as part of the Indian Residential Schools Settlement Agreement, to provide a permanent home for all the statements, documents and other materials the TRC would gather over its years of operation.

The NCTR ensures that:

▸ Survivors and their families have access to their own history

▸ educators can share the Residential School history with new generations of students

▸ researchers can delve more deeply into the Residential School experience

▸ the public can access historical records and other materials to help foster reconciliation and healing

▸ the history and legacy of the residential school system are never forgotten

▸ For more on the NCTR visit umanitoba.ca/nctr/

National Council for Reconciliation

In December 2016, Prime Minister Justin Trudeau announced the creation of a National Council for Reconciliation as part of his government's plans to advance reconciliation. An interim board of directors will begin developing recommendations on the scope and mandate of the council.

Imagine a Canada: Celebrating Youth Visions for Reconciliation

Imagine a Canada is a national essay and arts initiative through which young people can share their thoughts on the future of Canada.

nctr.ca/education_imagine.php

Legacy of Hope

The Legacy of Hope Foundation (LHF) is a national Indigenous charitable organization whose purpose is to educate, raise awareness and understanding of the legacy of Residential Schools, and support the ongoing healing process of Residential School Survivors. Fulfilling this mandate contributes toward reconciliation among generations of Indigenous peoples and all Canadians.

legacyofhope.ca/

Reconciliation Canada

Chief Dr. Robert Joseph often speaks to the need for each of us to create a Back Pocket Reconciliation Action Plan—something that reminds us of our definition of reconciliation and the ways we want to be part of reconciliation in our country.

It is designed to be:

▸ portable. Carry your Back Pocket Reconciliation Action Plan with you. Refer to it often.

▸ shareable. Spread the word! Let the world know how you're delivering change. Take a photo of your Back Pocket Reconciliation Action Plan to share on social media.

Follow the link to the action plan. Download and print it out (or make your own), fill it in, then share it with family and friends.

reconciliationcanada.ca/back-pocket-plan/

Here are some questions that might help you create your Back Pocket Reconciliation Action Plan.

▸ What action can you take today?

▸ What action can you take with your family?

▸ What action can you take at your school?

▶ What action can you take in your community?

Canadian Roots Exchange

Canadian Roots Exchange builds bridges between Indigenous and non-Indigenous youth in Canada by facilitating dialogue and strengthening relationships through leadership programs. They believe in a Canada where youth stand in solidarity to promote respect, understanding and reconciliation between Indigenous and non-Indigenous peoples.

canadianroots.ca/

#94DaysForReconciliation

The #94DaysForReconciliation campaign shares the 94 Calls to Action that came out of the final TRC report. Its goal is to keep the calls alive and relevant and to help viewers understand how the they are important to young people. Each day, for 94 days, there is a video posted, an article or a picture dedicated to the call to action of the day. Youth from across the country have contributed. Use the hashtag to check it out on YouTube. Maybe you'll even see someone you know!

Orange Shirt Day

Phyllis (Jack) Webstad wore a bright orange shirt with pride on her first day at Residential School in Williams Lake, BC, only to have it taken away, never to be seen again. Years later Phyllis created Orange Shirt Day, a day when you can honour Residential School Survivors and stand up against racism and bullying. It is one of the fastest-growing reconciliation projects in Canada.

Orange Shirt Day usually occurs on or around September 30. The date was chosen because it is the time of year when children were taken from their homes to Residential Schools. It is an opportunity to remind students and staff about policies that contribute to a respectful school community. Orange Shirt Day is also an opportunity for First Nations, local governments, schools and communities to come together in the spirit of reconciliation and hope for generations of children to come.

www.orangeshirtday.org/

The Kairos Blanket Exercise

The Blanket Exercise is a powerful activity that shares both the historic and contemporary relationship between Indigenous and non-Indigenous peoples in Canada. According to the Kairos website, "Blanket Exercise participants take on the roles of Indigenous peoples in Canada. Standing on blankets that represent the land, they walk through pre-contact, treaty-making, colonization and resistance."

kairosblanketexercise.org/

Project of Heart

Project of Heart was founded in 2007 by Ottawa secondary school teacher Sylvia Smith, who was outraged to discover that there were only sixty-four words pertaining to Residential Schools in her students' history textbook. Ms. Smith decided to do something—an act of reconciliation. She created an education tool to engage students in a deeper exploration of Indigenous traditions in Canada and the history of Indian Residential Schools.

Students, classes and schools create projects that show what they have learned about Residential Schools and reconciliation.

projectofheart.ca/

Truth and Reconciliation Reading Challenge

In April 2016, Jennifer Manuel launched an online campaign called the TRC Reading Challenge. By October 2016, almost 4,000 Canadians had signed up to read the final report of the TRC. "Take as long as you need to read it," states the challenge website. "It's a commitment, not a race."

trcreadingchallenge.com/

Red Man Laughing podcast: Reconciliation

Ryan McMahon is an Anishinabe/Métis comedian, writer and actor based in Treaty 1 territory (Winnipeg, Manitoba). Ryan uses his gifts to not only entertain but also make us think about our history, about the importance of land and water, about relationships, about so much…including reconciliation. For example, one of his quotes that rings true in my heart is: "Reconciliation is asking myself who my Ancestors were the day before they went to Residential School, then doing everything I can to return to that."

Ryan has dedicated Season 5 of the *Red Man Laughing* podcast to reconciliation. Do yourself a favour—put the *Red Man Laughing* podcast on your phone or computer, and get ready to laugh, be inspired and to think as well.

www.redmanlaughing.com

The Witness Blanket

Inspired by a woven blanket, the Witness Blanket is a national touring monument honouring the legacy of Residential Schools. It is a large-scale art installation, created by artist Carey Newman out of hundreds of items reclaimed from Residential Schools, churches, government buildings and traditional and cultural structures across Canada, including friendship centres, Band offices, treatment centres and universities. The Witness Blanket stands as a memorial to recognize the atrocities of the Indian Residential School era, honour the children and symbolize ongoing reconciliation.

witnessblanket.ca/

Photo: Melissa Welsh

Carey's Journey

Carey Newman is an Indigenous artist of Kwagiulth, Salish and British heritage. He is the creator of the Witness Blanket, a national monument honouring the legacy of Residential Schools. We met for breakfast, and over our meal he shared his powerful story with me.

"It started with my dad, and my relationship with him. We went to counselling, and that's where I learned about Residential School. I learned that he was really damaged there, and that I didn't have a dad. I was younger, in my early teens, when that happened, and it helped me understand my relationship a lot better and took the edge off a lot of things he said when he'd get grouchy.

"Later, when I was in college, I wrote a research essay about Residential School. This was before it was a national conversation. This was before many Survivors were willing to publicly talk, because it just wasn't part of what was happening. So I found a few who were willing to talk, and the things they disclosed were really powerful, and that laid the foundation for the passion that I have for the subject of reconciliation and the history of Residential Schools."

When he started to work on the Witness Blanket, he came up with a definition for reconciliation: "Every person is going to approach this in a different way, and every person will have a measurement within their heart or soul that will determine for them what reconciliation is. I don't think there is one blanket answer. When you read the definition of reconciliation, it is one of coming back, the reinstatement of the relationship. I have a problem with that because there wasn't really good relationships to begin with, so let's call it *conciliation*. We are coming to good relations rather than reinstating them.

"Reconciliation means whatever part of the process you are still in. If you are angry, that's fine. If you are ready to forgive, that's fine. Wherever you are at in your healing process, that's fine. As someone who spends a lot of time working in the field of reconciliation, I think we aren't there yet. When the education of our children is valued at the same level across the country, when our children are treated [with respect] by the social welfare system across the country, when we as Indigenous people have the same justice in the legal system, we will have equal ground both as victims and as perpetrators. When we resolve the question of land title, we will have equal ground. That's the starting point of reconciliation. Reconciliation really starts for me when we reach equal ground. Then it is about setting aside preconceptions. Many times these conversations include clean drinking water, and I don't think that is reconciliation. I think that is a human rights issue, a poverty issue, a social justice issue—not a reconciliation issue.

A detail from the Witness Blanket.
CAREY NEWMAN AND MEDIA ONE

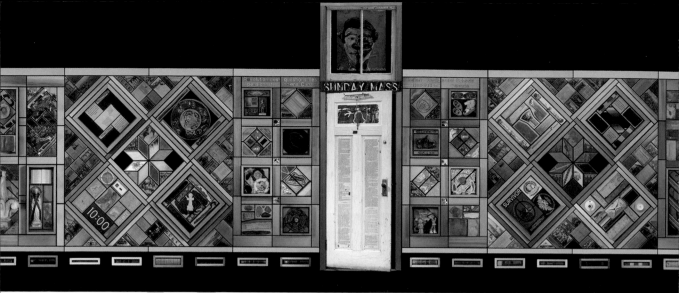

The Witness Blanket travels across Canada so as many people as possible can see it.
CAREY NEWMAN AND MEDIA ONE

Reflections

What do you think it was like for Carey to hold the Residential School items in his hands and decide where and how to place every item on the Witness Blanket?

In what ways do you think a national monument like the Witness Blanket is important?

"It's important to stand up for yourself and others, and that goes for all people. It's important to challenge misconceptions, not in an aggressive way, but to point out the misconceptions.

"I look forward to when we can all take pride in this country. Not the country Sir John A. Macdonald thought he was building, but what Canada really is. When we say Canada is a melting pot, that it's people from all over the world, *and* it is Indigenous people who were already here. When we embrace each other's cultures equally… that's where reconciliation is." ●

UNTIL OUR PATHS CROSS AGAIN…

As Maddy said earlier, awareness creates healing. After you've read this book, I hope you are much more aware of Canada's history. Again, not Indigenous history, but Canadian history. As well, I hope you are more aware of the important contributions the residential

> **"The blanket is a universal symbol of protection. For many of us, it identifies who we are and where we're from—we wear them in ceremony and give them as gifts. Blankets protect our young and comfort our elders."**
> **Carey Newman**

school Survivors and their families have made to our society through the work of the Truth and Reconciliation Commission. And I hope that all of this awareness fosters within you a desire to continue taking steps in your own journey of reconciliation.

We are coming to the end of our journey together. I know it is not the end of my journey, and I hope it is not the end of yours.

Writing this book has changed me in ways that are hard to describe. Many of you will be familiar with the story of how Raven brings the light, and you may also know that Raven is a trickster. Well, Raven also brings transformation…change within ourselves. I feel like Raven was with me through the months of writing this book…bringing more light and understanding as well as transformation.

First Nations mural art from Vancouver Island features Raven, who is often known as the trickster. SHUTTERSTOCK.COM

How was I transformed? Well, I have a deeper respect for my family members and Ancestors, who lived through so much of what was shared in the history chapter, including Residential Schools. Not only do I have a deeper respect for them, but I also understand why they are the way they are. I was and remain profoundly impacted by all of the interviews I did for this book, but especially the ones with the young people. I carry in my heart their wisdom, honesty and hope for our country. And I hug my children tighter! Had they been born even twenty-five years ago, they could be at Residential School, and I wouldn't be able to hug them or tell them I love them.

Vuntut Gwitchin First Nation member, Rachael Blake Elias, 13, rests after snowshoeing near Old Crow, YT.
DEDDEDA WHITE

Young people are vital to how we move forward.

Each of you.

Every single one of you.

We need you.

Being needed may feel like a burden, but it is the truth. It doesn't mean you have to become political activists or that your life has to revolve around reconciliation. It can be as simple as living your life based on the braid of sweetgrass.

A life in which you do your best to be honest.

Jingle dancers take part in a Pow Wow in Kahnawake, QC, 2016. SHUTTERSTOCK.COM

In which, whenever you can, you share the medicine of love, and in your relationships you strive for kindness and reciprocity.

In which you try to live your life as an act of reconciliation.

Kinanâskomitin

In my Nihiyaw (Cree) language, *kinanâskomitin* means so much more than "thank you!" I understand it to mean "I honour you for this time we have spent together and am grateful you are alive."

So this is what I'd like to say to you as our journey together comes to a close, at least for now. Kinanâskomitin!!!

All my relations,
Monique Gray Smith

Acknowledgments

I want to start by offering gratitude to the Lekwungen people for allowing me to be a visitor on their territory—to live here, play here, work here and, most important, raise my children here!

Kinanâskomitin (Cree for "thank you") to the Residential School Survivors for sharing their lived experiences with us. I can only imagine the courage and strength it has taken for you to share your stories. I am deeply humbled by your journeys, and I hope we are truly learning from you so that we never repeat the atrocities of the past. I acknowledge and thank everyone who contributed to *The Survivors Speak: A Report of the Truth and Reconciliation Commission of Canada*. This report, released in 2015, was instrumental in the writing of chapter two.

I offer much gratitude to my family, Rhonda, Sadie and Jaxson. Thank you for supporting me in everything I do, but especially in the writing of this book. The love and laughter you shared with me healed me when I came home, shattered by what I had been working on during the day. You are the reason for my being!

Thank you to my daughter, Sadie, who read each draft and provided me with important feedback that helped shape this book. You are wiser and smarter than you know!

Thank you to my son, Jaxson, who read the first page of the history chapter and simply put it down. That was the message I needed to write that chapter in a different way! Sometimes it is the small gestures that have a huge impact.

Many thanks to Margo D'Archangelo for all her support on this project! Thank you for sitting with me for hours as I mapped out and brainstormed the book. I appreciate all your time researching, and I acknowledge the impact some of the reading had on you! You have a beautiful heart, Margo!

Thanks to Kamille Tobin for the hours you spent transcribing the interviews and for the notes of encouragement you sent with every email.

Huge gratitude to those who allowed me to interview them. Thank you for sharing your thoughts, wisdom and hopes: Elder Diane Longboat, Elder Fred John, Craig Knight, Dr. Marie Wilson, Keith Matthew, Shelagh Rogers, Lisa Helps and Chastity Davis. The young people I talked to inspired me in ways that words cannot describe: Sahej, Maddy, Natasha, Mirabella, Gabe, Amelia, Amber, Jade and Liam. As well, thank you to the parents of these young people for helping organize the interviews.

Thank you to Selkirk Montessori School for sharing your space with us as we took photos for the book. Thank you to the youth who agreed to be in the photos: Ocean, Sahej, Bella, Tatiana, Frances, the two Sadies, Natasha, Maddy, Amy and Gabe.

Deep respect and gratitude to my editor, Sarah Harvey. I appreciate not only your knowledge in the actual editing of this book, but also the tenderness you extended to me. Thank you for knowing that this was not an easy book for me to write, and for all the ways you supported me!!! You have truly been a gift in this journey!

Much gratitude to Greg Younging for taking the time to review the book and for sharing his feedback and wisdom.

Thank you to Orca Book Publishers and specifically Andrew Wooldridge for asking me to write this book and for believing in me. I am grateful to Ruth Linka and Dayle Sutherland for their gentle and compassionate ways. Thank you to the Orca team for being allies in this journey of reconciliation.

Online Resources

Calls to Action, Truth and Reconciliation Commission of Canada:
nctr.ca/assets/reports/Calls_to_Action_English2.pdf

The Canadian Encyclopedia, "Residential Schools":
www.thecanadianencyclopedia.ca/en/article/residential-schools/

Gord Downie's *The Secret Path*:
www.youtube.com/watch?v=yGd764YU9yc

Honouring the Truth, Reconciling for the Future: Summary of the Final Report of the Truth and Reconciliation Commission of Canada:
www.trc.ca/websites/trcinstitution/File/2015/Honouring_the_Truth_Reconciling_for_the_Future_July_23_2015.pdf

Reconciliation Canada:
reconciliationcanada.ca/?gclid=CNmU49-CkNICFQ-dfgodJOoM5w

Truth and Reconciliation Commission final reports:
www.trc.ca/websites/trcinstitution/index.php?p=890

Truth and Reconciliation Commission FAQs:
www.trc.ca/websites/trcinstitution/index.php?p=10

Truth and Reconciliation Summit video:
www.banffcentre.ca/truth-and-reconciliation-summit

Truth: In My Own Words **(film project)**:
www.youtube.com/watch?v=TIqUwV1mwoQ

Reading List

Alexie, Robert Arthur. *Porcupines and China Dolls.* Penticton, BC: Theytus Books, 2009.

André, Julie-Ann, and Mindy Willett. *We Feel Good Out Here: Zhik gwaa'an, nakhwatthaiitat gwiinzii (The Land Is Our Storybook).* Calgary, AB: Fifth House Publishers, 2008.

Arnaktauyok, Germaine, and Gyu Oh. *My Name Is Arnaktauyok: The Life and Art of Germaine Arnaktauyok.* Iqaluit, NU: Inhabit Media, 2015.

Boyden, Joseph. *Wenjack.* Toronto, ON: Hamish Hamilton Canada, 2016.

Campbell, Nicola. *Shin-chi's Canoe.* Toronto, ON: Groundwood Books, 2008.

Downie, Gord, and Jeff Lemire. *Secret Path.* Toronto, ON: Simon & Schuster, 2016.

Dupuis, Jenny Kay, and Kathy Kacer. *I Am Not a Number.* Toronto, ON: Second Story Press, 2016.

Gray, Lynda. *First Nations 101.* Vancouver, BC: Adaawx Publishing, 2011.

Halfe, Louise Bernice. *Bear Bones and Feathers.* Regina, SK: Coteau Books, 1994.

Hill, Gord. *The 500 Years of Resistance Comic Book.* Vancouver, BC: Arsenal Pulp Press, 2010.

Jordan-Fenton, Christy, and Margaret Pokiak-Fenton. *Fatty Legs: A True Story.* Toronto, ON: Annick Press, 2010.

———. *Stranger at Home: A True Story.* Toronto, ON: Annick Press, 2011.

LaBoucane-Benson, Patti. *The Outside Circle: A Graphic Novel.* Toronto, ON: House of Anansi Press, 2015.

Loyie, Larry, with Constance Brissenden. *As Long as the Rivers Flow.* Toronto, ON: Groundwood Books, 2005.

———. *Goodbye Buffalo Bay.* Penticton, BC: Theytus Books, 2008.

Olsen, Sylvia, with Rita Moss and Ann Sam. *No Time to Say Goodbye: Children's Stories of Kuper Island Residential School.* Winlaw, BC: Sono Nis Press, 2001.

Robertson, David Alexander, and Scott B. Henderson. *Sugar Falls: A Residential School Story.* Winnipeg, MB: Highwater Press, 2012.

Sellars, Bev. *They Called Me Number One: Secrets and Survival at an Indian Residential School.* Vancouver, BC: Talonbooks, 2012.

Slipperjack, Ruby. *Dear Canada: These Are My Words: The Residential School Diary of Violet Pesheens.* Markham, ON: Scholastic Canada, 2016.

Smith, Monique Gray. *Tilly: A Story of Hope and Resilience.* Winlaw, BC: Sono Nis Press, 2014.

Sterling, Shirley. *My Name is Seepeetza.* Toronto, ON: Groundwood Books, 1992.

Van Camp, Richard. *Whistle.* Toronto, ON: Pearson Canada, 2015.

Vermette, Katherena. *Amik Loves School: A Story of Wisdom.* Winnipeg, MB: Portage & Main Press, 2015.

Glossary

Aboriginal—the term in the Constitution of Canada, and still used by many people, to describe First Nations (status and non-status), Métis and Inuit people.

ally—a person, group or nation that is linked with and works together with another person, group or nation for a shared purpose.

assimilation—the process whereby a person's or a group's culture becomes or is made to become like that of another group. The person or group with less power is almost always expected to change.

colonize—to send settlers to a place in order to establish political control over it. This is done by creating new governing systems and ways of living, being and doing that make the ways of those who were there before inferior. This creates unequal relationships between the colonizer and the Indigenous people.

Confederation—the process by which the British Colonies of Canada, Nova Scotia and New Brunswick were united into one Dominion of Canada on July 1, 1867. Eventually the other provinces and territories joined and created what we know as Canada today.

cultural genocide—destruction of the structures and practices, such as language, ceremonies and spiritual beliefs, that allow a racial, religious, ethnic or national group to continue as a group.

Elders—An Elder is often on older person who is considered wise because of their knowledge and understanding of the land, language, traditional ways, teachings, stories and ceremonies.

First Peoples—the descendants of the original people living in Canada.

First Nation—First Peoples identify themselves by the nation to which they belong (Dene, Nuu-chah-nulth, Mohawk, Cree, for example). The members of a nation sometimes share common values, traditions and practices rooted in their ancestral heritage. Today, many bands prefer to be known as First Nations.

genocide—deliberate and intended action to destroy a group of people.

honourary witness—someone who witnesses and remembers an event of historic significance and also shares what he or she saw, felt, heard and experienced.

Indian—a term used to describe the First Peoples of Canada up until the 1980s.

Indian Act—the body of Canadian laws that sets out federal government responsibilities for managing reserve lands, money and other resources. It was first passed in 1876 and has been altered several times since then.

Indian agent—the representative of the Department of Indian Affairs (now known as Indigenous and Northern Affairs Canada). Indian agents were in charge of many aspects of affairs in their area or the reserve(s) they were assigned to. The powers of the Indian agent were significant and influenced the lives of all First Nations people in their area.

Indian status—a person's legal status as an Indian, as defined by the Indian Act.

Indigenous—the term that is most commonly being used now to describe the First Peoples.

intergenerational Survivor—a child or grandchild of a Survivor, and anyone else who has been affected by the separation of generations of children from their families.

internalized racism— when people being discriminated against begin to adopt the racist attitudes and stereotypical beliefs about their own race.

Inuit—the word means "people" in Inuktitut (the Inuit language). In Canada, the word describes the First People who live in Nunavut, Northwest Territories and northern Quebec and Labrador.

matriarchal—describes a society in which the positions of power or respect are held by women, and women are highly regarded.

matrilineal—tracing family relationships through the female line, rather than the male line, meaning that children would inherit from their mother's side, not their father's.

Métis—people of First Nation and European ancestry who identify as being Métis and can link their heritage to the historic Red River settlement. The term has different historical and contemporary meanings, however, and is sometimes used to describe anyone of European-First Nation ancestry who identifies as Métis. Métis ancestors are most often Scottish, French, Ojibwe and Cree.

moral courage—the courage to take action, even if there will be consequences, because you feel it is the right thing to do.

oral traditions—communication whereby knowledge, ideas, stories and teachings are protected and shared verbally. Sharing may occur through conversation, storytelling or song and gets passed from one generation to another.

Potlatch—a ceremonial feast acknowledging important events such as births, deaths, marriages, etc. Gift giving and honouring of guests are integral aspects of the ceremony. Potlatch is not part of every First Nation's culture.

pre-contact—the time before Europeans arrived in Canada.

privilege—any unearned benefit, right, opportunity or advantage given to a person or a group because of their identity (class, race, age, gender, sex, etc.).

racism—discrimination and prejudice toward a person or people because of their race.

reciprocity—the mutual exchange of privilege, so that everyone benefits and has the same privileges, and people repay what another has provided to them.

reconciliation—the restoration and healing of a relationship. In Canada, this refers to the process taken on by the Truth and Reconciliation Commission to revitalize the relationship between the citizens of Canada (Indigenous and non-Indigenous), as well as the Nation-to-Nation relationships with the Government of Canada.

resilience—the ability to bounce back from challenging or difficult times in our lives.

The Seven Sacred Teachings—also known as the Seven Grandfather Teachings—is a set of traditional teachings which originated with the Anishanaabe (a group of culturally related Indigenous peoples in Canada and the United States). The teachings are followed and practiced by many other Indigenous peoples in both countries.

sterilization—to eliminate a person's ability to have children by changing or removing his or her reproductive organs.

systemic racism—when systems (like schools or the justice system) are supported and maintained by policies, practices and procedures that result in some people receiving better or worse treatment than others because of their race.

Traditional Knowledge Keepers—people (often Elders) who know, hold, protect and share traditional and local knowledge. Often traditional knowledge has been orally passed for generations, through stories, legends, rituals and songs.

List of Residential Schools (courtesy of the NCTR)

Alberta Residential Schools

Assumption (Hay Lakes), *Assumption*

Blue Quills (Saddle Lake, Sacred Heart, formerly Lac la Biche), *St. Paul*

Crowfoot (St. Joseph's, St. Trinité), *Cluny*

Desmarais (Wabisca Lake, St. Martins, Wabisca Roman Catholic), *Desmarais-Wabasca*

Edmonton (Poundmaker, formerly Red Deer Industrial), *St. Albert*

Ermineskin, *Hobbema*

Fort Vermilion (St. Henry's), *Fort Vermilion*

Grouard (St. Bernard's, Lesser Slave Lake Roman Catholic), *Grouard*

Holy Angels (Fort Chipewyan , École des Saints-Anges), Fort Chipewyan

Joussard IRS (St. Bruno's), *Joussard*

Lac la Biche (Notre Dame des Victoire, predecessor to Blue Quills), *Lac La Biche*

Lesser Slave Lake (St. Peter's), *Lesser Slave Lake*

Morley (Stony), *Morley*

Old Sun, *Gleichen*

Sacred Heart (Brocket), *Brocket*

St. Albert (Youville), *Youville*

St. Augustine (Smoky River), *Smoky River*

St. Cyprian's (Queen Victoria's Jubilee Home, Peigan), *Brocket*

St. Joseph's Residential School (High River, Dunbow), *High River*

St. Mary's (Blood, Immaculate Conception), *Cardston*

St. Paul's (Blood, Anglican/Church of England), *Cardston*

Sarcee (St. Barnabas), *T'suu Tina*

Sturgeon Lake (Calais, St. Francis Xavier), *Calais*

Wabasca Anglican/Church of England (St. John's), *Wabasca*

Whitefish Lake (St. Andrew's), *Whitefish Lake*

Gordon's School in Punnichy, SK. THE GENERAL SYNOD ARCHIVES, ANGLICAN CHURCH OF CANADA

British Columbia Residential Schools

Ahousat, *Ahousat*

Alberni IRS, *Port Alberni*

Anahim Lake Dormitory (September 1968 to June 1977), *Anahim Lake*

Cariboo (St. Joseph's, William's Lake), *Williams Lake*

Christie (Clayquot, Kakawis), *Tofino*

Coqualeetza, *Chilliwack/Sardis*

Cranbrook (St. Eugene's, Kootenay), *Cranbrook*

Kamloops, *Kamloops*

Kitimaat, *Kitimaat*
Kuper Island, *Kuper Island*
Lejac (Fraser Lake), *Fraser Lake*
Lower Post, *Lower Post*
Port Simpson (Crosby Home for Girls), *Port Simpson*
St. George's (Lytton), *Lytton*
St. Mary's (Mission), *Mission*
St. Michael's (Alert Bay Girls' Home, Alert Bay Boys' Home), *Alert Bay*
St. Paul's IRS (Squamish, North Vancouver), *North Vancouver*
Sechelt Residential School, *Sechelt*

Cross Lake Indian Residential School, Cross Lake, MB, 1939. LAC 4673884

Manitoba Residential Schools
Assiniboia (Winnipeg), *Winnipeg*
Birtle, *Birtle*
Brandon, *Brandon*
Churchill Vocational Centre, *Churchill*
Cross Lake (St. Joseph's, Jack River Annex—predecessor to Notre Dame Hostel), *Cross Lake*
Dauphin (McKay), *The Pas/Dauphin*
Elkhorn (Washakada), *Elkhorn*

Fort Alexander (Pine Falls), *Fort Alexander*
Guy (Guy Hill, Clearwater, The Pas, formerly Sturgeon Landing, SK), *The Pas*
Norway House United Church, *Norway House*
Notre Dame Hostel (Norway House Roman Catholic, Jack River Hostel, replaced Jack River Annex at Cross Lake), *Norway House*
Pine Creek (Camperville), *Camperville*
Portage la Prairie, *Portage la Prairie*
Sandy Bay, *Marius*

Northwest Territories Residential Schools
Akaitcho Hall (Yellowknife Vocational School), *Yellowknife*
Aklavik Roman Catholic (Immaculate Conception), *Aklavik*
Aklavik Anglican (All Saints), *Aklavik*
Deh Cho Hall (Lapointe Hall), *Fort Simpson*
Federal Hostel at Fort Franklin, *Fort Franklin*
Fort McPherson (Fleming Hall), *Fort McPherson*
Fort Providence Boarding Home (Sacred Heart), *Fort Providence*
Fort Resolution Residence (St. Joseph's), *Fort Resolution*
Fort Simpson Anglican (Bompas Hall), *Fort Simpson*
Fort Simpson Roman Catholic (Lapointe Hall), *Fort Simpson*
Fort Smith (Breynat Hall), *Fort Smith*
Fort Smith (Grandin College), *Fort Smith*
Hay River (St. Peter's), *Hay River*

Inuvik Roman Catholic (Grollier Hall), *Inuvik*
Inuvik Anglican Hostel (Stringer Hall), *Inuvik*

Nova Scotia Residential Schools
Shubenacadie, *Shubenacadie*

Nunavut Residential Schools
Chesterfield Inlet (Turquetil Hall), *Chesterfield Inlet*
Coppermine (Tent Hostel), *Coppermine*
Federal Hostel at Baker Lake/Qamani'tuaq, *Qamani'tuaq/Qamanittuaq*
Federal Hostel at Belcher Islands, *Sanikiluaq*
Federal Hostel at Broughton Island/ Qikiqtarjuaq, *Qikiqtarjuaq*
Federal Hostel at Cambridge Bay, *Cambridge Bay*
Federal Hostel at Cape Dorset/Kinngait, *Kinngait*
Federal Hostel at Eskimo Point/Arviat, *Arviat*
Federal Hostel at Frobisher Bay (Ukkivik), *Iqaluit*
Federal Hostel at Igloolik/Iglulik, *Igloolik/ Iglulik*
Federal Hostel at Lake Harbour, *Kimmirut*
Federal Hostel at Pangnirtung (Pangnirtang), *Pangnirtung/Panniqtuuq*
Federal Hostel at Pond Inlet/Mittimatalik, *Mittimatalik*

Ontario Residential Schools
Bishop Horden Hall (Moose Fort, Moose Factory), *Moose Factory Island*
Cecilia Jeffrey (Kenora, Shoal Lake), *Kenora*
Chapleau (St. John's), *Chapleau*
Cristal Lake, *Northwestern Ontario*
Fort Frances (St. Margaret's), *Fort Frances*
Fort William (St. Joseph's), *Fort William*
McIntosh, *McIntosh*
Mohawk Institute, *Brantford*
Mount Elgin (Muncey, St. Thomas), *Munceytown*
Pelican Lake (Pelican Falls), *Sioux Lookout*
Poplar Hill, *Poplar Hill*
St. Anne's (Fort Albany), *Fort Albany*
St. Mary's (Kenora, St. Anthony's), *Kenora*
Shingwauk, *Sault Ste. Marie*
Spanish Boys' School (Charles Garnier, St. Joseph's, formerly Wikwemikong Industrial), *Spanish*
Spanish Girls' School (St. Joseph's, St. Peter's, St. Anne's, formerly Wikwemikong Industrial), *Spanish*
Stirland Lake (Wahbon Bay Academy), *Stirland Lake*

Québec Residential Schools
Amos (St. Marc-de-Figuery), *Amos*
Fort George (St. Phillip's), *Fort George*
Fort George (St. Joseph's Mission, Residence Couture, Sainte-Thérèse-de-l'Énfant-Jésus), *Fort George*
Federal Hostel at George River, *Kangirsualujjuaq*
Federal Hostel at Great Whale River (Poste-de-la-Baleine, Kuujjuaraapik), *Kuujjuaraapik/Whapmagoostui*

Mistassini Hostels, *Mistassini*

Federal Hostel at Payne Bay (Bellin),
   Kangirsuk

Federal Hostel at Port Harrison (Inoucdjouac,
   Innoucdouac), *Inukjuak*

La Tuque, *La Tuque*

Point Bleue, *Point Bleue*

Sept-Îles (Seven Islands, Notre Dame,
   Maliotenam), *Sept-Îles*

Oblate Fathers' Mission School,
Fort George, QC, ca 1946. LAC 3199031

Saskatchewan Residential Schools

Battleford, *Battleford*

Beauval (Lac la Plonge), *Beauval*

Cote Improved Federal Day School (for the
   period September 1928 to June 1940)
   Kamsack

Crowstand, *Kamsack*

File Hills, *Balcarres*

Fort Pelly, *Fort Pelly*

Gordon's, *Gordon's Reserve, Punnichy*

Lac La Ronge, *La Ronge (Later transferred to
   Prince Albert)*

Lebret (Qu'Appelle, Whitecalf, St. Paul's High
   School), *Lebret*

Marieval (Cowesess, Crooked Lake), *Grayson*

Muscowequan (Lestock, Touchwood), *Lestock*

Onion Lake Anglican, *Onion Lake
   (Later transferred to Prince Albert)*

Prince Albert (Onion Lake Church of
   England, St. Alban's, All Saints, St.
   Barnabas, Lac La Ronge), *Prince Albert*

Regina, *Regina*

Round Lake, *Stockholm*

St. Anthony's (Onion Lake Roman Catholic),
   Onion Lake

St. Michael's (Duck Lake), *Duck Lake*

St. Phillip's, *Kamsack*

Sturgeon Landing (predecessor to Guy Hill,
   MB), *Sturgeon Landing*

Thunderchild (Delmas), *Delmas*

Yukon Residential Schools

Carcross (Chooulta), *Carcross*

Coudert Hall (Whitehorse Hostel/Student
   Residence—predecessor to Yukon Hall),
   Whitehorse

St. Paul's Hostel (September 1920 to June
   1943), *Dawson City*

Shingle Point (Predecessor to All Saints,
   Aklavik, NWT), *Shingle Point*

Whitehorse Baptist Mission, *Whitehorse*

Yukon Hall (Whitehorse/Protestant Hostel),
   Whitehorse

Index

Page numbers in **bold** indicate an image; there may also be text related to the same topic on that page

Photo: Centric Photography

Monique Gray Smith is a mixed-heritage woman of Cree, Lakota and Scottish descent and is the proud mom of twins. Monique's first published novel, *Tilly: A Story of Hope and Resilience,* won the 2014 Burt Award for First Nations, Métis and Inuit Literature. Monique's career has focused on fostering paradigm shifts that emphasize the strength and resiliency of the First Peoples in Canada. She is well known for her storytelling, spirit of generosity and focus on resilience. Monique has been sober and involved in her healing journey for over twenty-six years and lives with her family on Lekwungen territory in Victoria, British Columbia. For more information, visit www.moniquegraysmith.com.